VIA Folios 184

Carmela Perciante, Laura LaGuardia,
Laura Manfredi, Vincenzo LaGuardia, circa 1924

It Takes a Lifetime to Learn How to Live

Published by Bordighera Press, an imprint of the John D. Calandra Italian American Institute of Queens College, The City University of New York.

25 West 43rd Street, 17th Floor, New York, NY 10036

All rights reserved. Parts of this book may be reprinted only by written permission from the publisher, and may not be reproduced for publication in media of any kind, except in quotations for the purposes of literary reviews.

This is a true story, though some names have been changed.

Library of Congress Control Number: 2025942207

The title *It Takes a Lifetime to Learn How to Live* can be traced back to the Roman philosopher Seneca.

> *Professores aliarum artium vulgo multique sunt, quasdam vero ex his pueri admodum ita percepisse visi sunt tu etiam praecipere possent: vivere tota vita discendum est et, quod magis fortasse miraberis, tota vita discendum est mori.*

> "There are many teachers of other arts, and some of these seem to have been so thoroughly learned by children that they can even teach them; but to live is learned throughout life, and, what perhaps you will wonder at, to die is learned throughout life."

> Seneca, *On the Shortness of Life* (*De Brevitate Vitae*), c. 49 AD

Cover photograph (Woman) by iStock.com/lcodacci, illustration (Ocean) by iStock.com/Pobytov

Cover design by Lauren Giordano
Interior sketches by George Burroughs

© 2025, Libby Cataldi

VIA Folios 184
ISBN 978-1-59954-239-3

It Takes a Lifetime to Learn How to Live

An Italian American Story of Coming Home

Libby Cataldi

BORDIGHERA PRESS

Talvolta se mi accosto a questa terra, ne ho un urto impetuoso che mi rapisce come un'acqua in piena e vuol sommergermi. Una voce, un odore bastano a prendermi e buttarmi chi sa dove. Son fatto pietra, umidità, letame, succhio di frutto, vento.

Sometimes, when I approach this land, I feel a powerful jolt that sweeps me away like a flood and threatens to overwhelm me. A voice, a smell is enough to grab me and throw me who knows where. I am made of stone, moisture, manure, fruit pulp, wind.

    CESARE PAVESE, *FERIA D'AGOSTO*

* * *

Walking, I am listening to a deeper way.
Suddenly all my ancestors are behind me. Be still, they say.
    Watch and listen.
You are the result of the love of thousands.

    LINDA HOGAN, *DWELLINGS: A SPIRITUAL HISTORY OF THE LIVING WORLD*

To Nonna,
who taught me how to love.

To Mom,
who taught me how to forgive.

To Iysa and Monroe,
who carry our story forward.

Table of Contents

Prologue	11
Chapter 1: Vomit and Get on the Plane	17

ITALY

Chapter 2: The Refusal	33
Chapter 3: *Fare una Bella Figura*	38
Chapter 4: Cortona	42
Chapter 5: Study Italian, Bella	48
Chapter 6: Getting Ready for Rotondella	52

PITTSBURGH

Chapter 7: Carmela	63
Chapter 8: Carmela's Ring	74
Chapter 9: Laura	81
Chapter 10: Laura Remembers	91
Chapter 11: Laura's Secrets: Mafia, *Malocchio*, and the Missing Year	98

ROTONDELLA

Chapter 12: Thelma and Louise	111
Chapter 13: Giambattista's Inn	123
Chapter 14: The Search	129
Chapter 15: Carmela Perciante?	140
Chapter 16: No Mafia in Basilicata	152
Chapter 17: Via Cervaro	157
Chapter 18: Goodbye, Rotondella	163

PITTSBURGH

Chapter 19: Letting Nonna Go — 173
Chapter 20: Laura's Letting Go — 186

FLORENCE

Chapter 21: Life in Florence — 207

Epilogue — 211

Acknowledgments — 213
About the Author — 217

Prologue

1959

Comfortable as a priest before the altar, Carmela stands at her stove. Her right arm moves in familiar circles as she stirs rich red *sugo* with a wooden spoon—the spoon that never hits me. While she cooks, she moves her lips slowly in prayer. The scent of her heavenly tomato-and-garlic sauce quiets me, fills me with peace.

My grandmother is my North Star, my safe port in many childhood storms. Strong. Independent. She sweeps the snow from her sidewalk wearing only a sweater, makes her own wine, cans her own tomatoes, strings her own peppers to dry in the basement, and finds edible dandelions for salads in the yard. She is the matriarch of *la famiglia,* whose grown sons stop by every night after work to eat at her table before going to their own homes to eat again.

She can't read or write—not in Italian, not in English—but she's the smartest person I know. She teaches me how to eat pasta, how to cook, how to pray, and she knows how to protect those she loves.

She isn't afraid of anyone, not even my father. I will never forget the day she almost slit his throat.

We were playing, Nonna and I, Steal the Pile, the perfect game for an immigrant grandmother who worked in the fields and never went to school. The rules were simple: Match a card in your hand with a card of the same value that was face up in the center of the table. With each trick won, the player piled her cards in front of her, with the top card visible. You could steal someone's pile with a card of the same value.

I gave Nonna a challenging smile. "I have almost all the cards. This time, I'm going to win!" Glancing over the rim of her glasses, she returned my smile as she leaned forward. *"Uffa,"* she chuckled, "look what I do," as she scooped up my entire mountain of cards as naturally as she stirred a pot of tomato sauce.

And then the kitchen screen door banged open. My mother burst in. Her dark hair disheveled, her eyes red, she was looking around a little wildly, as if scared or trying to find a bolt-hole. I knew something terrible had happened for her to make this abrupt, unexpected entrance into Nonna's house. Even as Mom caught my eyes on her and pulled down her shirtsleeve to cover her upper arm, I had seen it already, the long, vivid imprint of a hand on her upper arm. I was eight. I knew a lot already, so much more than my parents thought I knew. I recognized the mark on her arm—my father's hand.

But it was her mother she wanted. Out came a torrent of words in whispers, telling Nonna, in a tight, breaking voice, what had happened. Nonna listened in silence. Her eyes narrowed and her jaw clenched. My mother opened the cellar door and fled downstairs to the bathroom. Nonna sat quietly, hands in her lap, palms facing the ceiling. She stared straight ahead. In her stillness, I could feel a storm gathering force in her, like the quiet before a tornado.

Mom's arrival had ended our game. I wedged the cards back into their red-and-white Bicycle box, walked into the dining room, and put it into the cabinet where Nonna stored her special dishes, the ones she used for Sunday family dinners.

Then I heard the slam of a car door outside the house. Peering out the window, I could see Dad hurrying across the lawn. He was dressed for work and wore a suit, but his tie was undone and loose around the open collar of his white shirt. When he reached the thirteen steps leading to Nonna's front porch, his long, athletic legs scaled them two at a time.

I knew our problems were about to get worse.

I peeked into the kitchen where Nonna had already turned her body toward the door. Her palms were still facing up, but her hands were now perched several inches above her legs, as if preparing for some action.

"Carmela," Dad called through the screen door. "I'd like to talk with Laura. I see her car out front." He didn't try to open the door, but continued, "I missed her at home and . . ."

Nonna had already grabbed a butcher cleaver that lay next to the sink. "*Teggia accir*," she hissed as she gripped the knife in her right hand, raised it above her head, and blasted through the screen door. *I kill you.*

Dad charged down the steps with Nonna on his heels, closing in. He fled to the far side of the car, placed his open hands on the roof, poised to dodge. From where he stood, he could see both Nonna and the house.

I ran onto the porch and froze. My father was a soldier, a Marine. I had never seen him run from anyone. My beloved nonna had become a stranger to me, wielding a cleaver as my father crouched along the car to shield himself from her. I watched, terrified. Confused. Scared. Pee trickled down my legs.

Dad glanced up and saw me, standing alone and gaping at the scene. He must have recognized my fear, or maybe he felt humiliated because he was running from Nonna, but whatever the reason, he laughed—a deep laugh—trying to make light of the situation. "Carmela, what's wrong? Don't say you want to kill me! What's gotten into you?"

She stopped in front of the driver's door, lifted the cleaver onto the roof, and banged the handle onto the metal. *Thump. Thump. Thump.* Her focus was intense and solely on Dad. I heard the pounding of the knife—*thump*—and the quiet threat of her words.

"*Teggia accir.*"

Her intentions were clear. She moved cautiously, one step at a time, sideways and to her left, beginning to circle the car, never taking her eyes off Dad. With each step she took toward him, he moved sideways and away from her with the same step-by-step movement, never taking his eyes off the knife.

Nonna stood at the front of the car, and Dad was behind the trunk. A few more steps and Nonna stood where Dad had been, and he was now at the driver's side. He yanked open the door, jumped in, turned on the ignition, and the engine roared. He sped away. In an instant, his car disappeared around the corner, leaving nothing but exhaust fumes in his wake.

Nonna lowered the cleaver to her side. She stood in the now empty street and glanced around to check if anyone had seen what had just happened. I did the same and saw no one. With her back straight and her chin high, she climbed the stairs back to Mom and me.

I opened the screen door for her, searching her eyes for some direction, for some way to make sense of what I had just seen. She touched my face gently with the hand that wasn't holding the butcher knife and slid tender fingers down my cheek. In the kitchen, she dropped the cleaver into the sink and sat next to my mom, who was collapsed into herself at the table, her head folded onto her arms, weeping.

Nonna looked at me and nodded her head toward the porch, as if to say, *Give me some time alone with your mamma.* I climbed onto the porch swing and wrapped my arms around my torso in an attempt to comfort myself. I willed my heart to quit racing, even as I felt the sickening taste of vomit climbing into my throat. I prayed, *Our Father, who art in heaven . . .*

My prayer was interrupted by the familiar sound of water filling up a pot. Looking to my right and into the window that was over the sink, I could see the thin, spiderweb strings of the net that held Nonna's gray hair in place and her tortoiseshell glasses that had slipped halfway down her nose. Her face, etched with wrinkles, looked severe, especially around her mouth where her lips were pressed into one thin and determined line.

When the pasta was ready, she called me to the table. But Nonna's elixir against pain—the comforting aroma of tomato sauce and the sweet taste of spaghetti sprinkled with freshly grated parmigiano cheese—were powerless to diminish what had just happened. Three generations of women sat in silence. Mom pushed spaghetti from one side of the shallow bowl to the other. Nonna offered a small glass of her homemade red wine, but Mom never touched it. I found it difficult to eat, but I knew that would upset Nonna, so I forced down the pasta.

Abruptly, Mom stood. "I have to leave. The boys. They don't know where I am. Fred is outside. Teddy . . . he's with a neighbor," she stammered. "I'm not home. They'll see my car is gone. They'll be worried."

Her face was angled toward Nonna, but her eyes darted from side to side as if she were trapped. I think she was sorry she had come. I think she regretted that she had gotten Nonna involved, and that I had seen what I'm sure she never wanted me to see. She didn't need to say these things, but I could read her slouched back, her heavy shoulders, her hands as they twisted around each other, and her eyes that never looked at me.

Without a word, Nonna followed her to the door, reached up, and made the sign of the cross three times on Mom's forehead. This was her holy protection.

After my mother left, I looked at Nonna's face: the set of her jaw, the wrinkles around her mouth, and especially the eyes that I knew as well as I knew my own. What was she thinking? What was she going to do? And how did she become a woman who could chase a Marine, who had fought at the Battle of Guadalcanal, out of her house with a butcher knife? I knew she was raised in poverty in a barren mountain village in Southern Italy called Rotondella. Was that where she learned this primal sense of standing up against anyone who threatened those she loved?

I didn't ask these questions, and I knew we would never talk about this episode. This was her way: Don't say a bad word about family. I picked up the plates to clear the table, but she took them from me and told me to get out the playing cards again. As I watched her deal the hand, I felt proud to be her granddaughter. My grandmother was a woman who knew her strength so well that she knew how to act from the heart when a member of her precious family needed her.

In a few minutes, back into the spirit of the game and trying to outwit Nonna, I almost wondered whether it had really happened. But it had happened, and I have remembered it. The thing that stays with me most is how quickly Nonna went from being a fearless warrior on the battlefield to a loving, wily, card-playing grandmother. She knew what the situation demanded and gave it. She had that kind of range.

*

Forty years later, when I was married and had two teenage sons, fear took over my life: Divorce, my older son's heroin addiction, and breast cancer were crushing me. I was ground down and didn't know what to do to save my family, help my son, or heal myself. When I relived that distant scene in Pittsburgh, I felt the pull of Nonna's fearlessness. I remembered how she acted with such power. I thought about her independence. Her strength. I hoped that I had her spirit in me—the unflinching courage to fight back, protect, and defend. I wanted to see the land that gave her birth, feel the dirt, discover the roots of her strength firsthand. I needed to learn the things that had been most dear to her, and to make them—the things that mattered most—my own.

Carmela held the key to my survival.

Chapter 1: Vomit and Get on the Plane

Thirty-two years later

Our home in Maryland was robbed. In 1991, when my sons, Jeremy and Jeffrey, were entering sixth and eighth grades, the three of us returned from a school shopping trip to find the front door hanging open. Without considering that someone could still be in the house, we made a quick survey and found no one and no apparent damage. However, all electronic equipment—Nintendo, electric guitar, tape players, movie camera, video recorders—was gone. The master bedroom, where my husband, Tim, and I slept, was untouched, but the boys' rooms were ransacked. In the end, there was nothing to do but call the police, file our losses with insurance, and better protect our home. The police analyzed the break-in and thought that it could have been the work of kids, maybe even older friends or acquaintances of Jeff's. We had a carpenter repair the front door, add a deadbolt, and secure the sliding glass windows with bars. Life went on.

I chalked up the burglary to the fact that our home was nestled in the woods and had two driveways—one exiting onto the public county road and the other onto a quiet, private cul-de-sac in our community—which made entrance and exit easy. Most of the day, the house sat empty. Tim and I were at work, and the boys attended school and often stayed for after-school activities. Tim was a successful businessman who, with two other men, founded and owned an environmental consulting firm. I held a doctorate in education from the University of Pittsburgh and had a teaching career, but when our sons were born, I wanted to stay home. Tim's income allowed me to be a full-time mom, and his absence from family events due to working long hours or traveling seemed to be the price of successful entrepreneurship.

When both boys reached elementary school age, I returned to work and eventually became Head of The Calverton School, where both Jeff and Jeremy were students. School became like a second family, where the three of us spent our days together. But life, even a good life, can go off the rails.

Two years after that first burglary, we were robbed again. This time when the boys and I came home after school, we found a boot mark stamped on the front door directly above the handle, where someone had kicked it open so forcefully that the door was ripped out of its wooden frame. This time we left the house immediately and called the police. When they arrived, we found that the master bedroom had been rifled. My jewelry had been apparently carried away in one of the pillowcases from our bed. The electronics that we had bought as replacements were gone, as was Tim's Les Paul guitar, which had survived the first theft. This job was done by more expert thieves.

Our home seemed to be an obvious target, so this time we contacted a burglar alarm company and arranged for a home security system to be installed. When the installation date was still two weeks off, on a Friday night while Tim was still at work, Jeremy needed to go to the library to find reference materials for his science fair project. Jeff, who was now in tenth grade, happily drove him. They left after dinner, around six thirty, and assured me they would be back soon. In the shorter days of February, it was already dark and, as I worked in my second-floor office overlooking the woods, I heard a banging sound that seemed as if it was coming from downstairs. I wished I was not alone. Although anxious, I tried to continue my work. Then I heard a scraping sound, whispering voices, at the front door or maybe coming from the living room windows.

Was I imagining things?

There was no car in our garage or driveway, so it was possible that someone could consider the house empty. Pretending that Tim was home in the hope of scaring off whomever might be within earshot—if someone was within earshot—I yelled loudly down the hall steps that led to the foyer, "Tim, will you come here, please? I need help with something." Then I sat quietly, listening intently. For ten minutes I sat frozen in my desk chair, alert for any sound. Although I didn't hear anything more, my nerves were now on edge. With two previous break-ins and no one home with me, I began to panic.

I recognized this fear: the tightness in my chest, the inability to breathe comfortably, and the pounding of my heart. I knew its source as a childhood story that was so frightening in my imagination that even as an adult, at any reasonable anxiety for my safety, it would reappear and intensify my fears in the present until I could barely think. The story came out of the time when, as a child, I often visited old Mrs. Wagner, a neighbor who lived alone and was one of the few people on our street who wasn't Italian. One evening, she warned me, "A convict from the penitentiary in McKees Rocks escaped last night. He could be in this area wandering around. He might even come to your house."

"He can't hurt me," I bragged, as only a seven-year-old girl can brag about her dad. "My dad's home and he's strong. He was a Marine."

"Oh, but this prisoner is a crazy man. He can put a ladder up to your bedroom window and climb in and get you. Your father would never know." She nodded emphatically, tilting her head toward me as if to drive home her point.

"I have screens on my windows, so the crazy man can't get in."

"Oh, but he can, my dear," she lectured sternly. "He has silent screen snippers that will cut through your screens without a sound."

That night, and for many years afterward, I closed and locked my bedroom windows.

This fear of the crazy man was deeply embedded in me as a child. As I grew into a woman, I tried to leave it behind, but such fears are smoldering fires. My old fears rushed up to fuel this new one.

I called Tim.

He answered on the fifth ring. "Where are you?" I asked immediately.

"I'm at work, Mary," he replied. My formal name is Mary Elizabeth, and he was the only person in the world who called me Mary. "Where else would I be?" He laughed.

"It's dark and it's eight fifteen on Friday night. When are you coming home?" I asked, trying to keep my voice calm.

"I have a lot to do, so much in fact that I might have to come into the office over the weekend. If not, I'll definitely have to work from home."

"Tim," my voice sharpened as I confessed, "I hear noises downstairs. I'm afraid. It's probably nothing, but the boys aren't here. They went to the library. I'm alone . . . I know you're busy . . . but I'd like you to come home. I'd feel safer if you were here. Please."

A pause. I heard him huff with frustration. "You're imagining things. The alarm system will be installed soon. No one in his right mind would rob a house after it's just been robbed. Settle down and relax. I'm busy. I have work to do."

I looked out the window in front of my desk and saw nothing but darkness. I heard the rustling trees and felt the walls closing in on me. Of course I knew the crazy man who haunted my childhood wasn't outside. But maybe someone else was.

"The boys are out and probably met friends at the library," I said, trying to keep my voice steady so Tim would think I was still reasonable. "I know you're busy and I know you think I'm overreacting, but I'd feel more secure if you were on your way. Why don't you bring your work home?"

His response was quicker this time. "Why don't you go next door to Louise's house and stay with her until the boys come back? Or call Fran from Calverton and ask her to come and sit with you. I bet she'd help."

Angered by his blatant lack of concern for my safety, I stung back, "This isn't something for Louise or Fran. I'd have to walk outside in the dark with a flashlight, down our long driveway, and up another to get to Louise's. Fran is at least forty minutes away. They're not my husband. I need my husband. I need you."

He raised his voice and countered, "Well, I'm like Fran and it would take me at least forty minutes to get there, so I'm no real help." A pause, and then he said with finality, "Listen, you'll need to do something else, call someone else. I'm not coming home."

"I'm afraid," I said softly. Tears welled. "I'm asking you to come home. Please."

Silence. Dead silence. I could barely hear him breathe.

"Tim?" I said to spur a response. No answer, but I heard papers being rustled. He was still on the phone.

On my desk, I had a pack of yellow sticky notes, and I pulled one off, rubbed my thumb across the top to secure it to the desk, and, while I held the receiver in my left hand, picked up a pencil and started writing: 1, 2, 3 . . . I decided that I would write up to sixty and, if Tim hadn't said a word by the time I wrote the numeral 60, I would hang up the phone.

I continued: 7, 8, 9 . . . Looking out into the black night, my mind wandered through past times when I had needed help and asked Tim. I thought about last winter when my car broke down on my way to a conference where I was the keynote speaker. Snow was beginning to fall as I sat stranded on the side of a deserted country road in southern Anne Arundel County. I called Tim. He listened as I explained what had happened. "What am I supposed to do? I'm at work and it's rush hour. I can't even get to you in time for your speech. Call Robert Lee. He sold you the car and he'll know what to do." He was off the phone before I could object. I called Robert Lee, who must have heard the tension in my voice because his response was immediate: "Don't worry. I'll get somebody to you right away. Just sit tight." Within twenty minutes, a tow truck arrived to my rescue. Not only did the driver load the car onto the trailer, he drove an additional ten miles out of his way to take me to the dinner, where I arrived just in time to speak. As I stood at the podium in front of four hundred people, I took a deep breath and willed my heart to quit pounding. Soon, I found my rhythm, and the speech was well received. After the event, Tim came and picked me up. He was forty minutes late.

19, 20, 21 . . . Tim and I met when I was seventeen years old and he was twenty-one, during my freshman year at Indiana University of Pennsylvania. I was pursuing a degree in education because my dad, an Italian patriarch, dictated—as if his words were Canon Law—that he would pay for college on two conditions: one, that I would attend a school within a one-hour drive of Pittsburgh, and two, that I would become a teacher or a nurse. "Your real job in life is to be a mother, and with either of these professions, you can work your schedule around your children. Sons are different. Your brothers will be breadwinners. You won't." Chemistry wasn't my strong suit, so the decision was clear.

One weekend, I was at a Kappa Delta Rho fraternity party and met Tim. He had graduated with a bachelor's degree in biology and environmental science and had a job with the Pennsylvania Department of Environmental Protection, but he still spent time on campus because he had a lot of friends in his fraternity. He was tall, thin, and handsome as he leaned against the wall and played the guitar while friends gathered around singing. Tim sang the melody, and I sang harmony as we blended our voices to Bob Dylan's "House of the Rising Sun" and The Everly Brothers' "All I Have to Do Is Dream." For our first date, he arrived in his parents' cool, navy-blue Pontiac GTO, wearing jeans, a white button-down shirt, and a dark-blue mohair sweater with the sleeves cut off. We climbed a mountain, and I saw my first shooting star.

34, 35, 36 . . . We laughed together during those early years while I was still in college. He could really *cut a rug* as we danced to the Temptations, the Four Tops, The Vogues, and The Drifters. My sorority voted him Man of the Year because he helped haul things in his car and drove us wherever we needed to go in his purple convertible. He taught me to fish for freshwater trout and to shoot a rifle. We golfed together. The saying *opposites attract* described us: He was quiet and shy, while I was extroverted and emotional. Before we married, I made a pro-and-con list. The pro side was filled with activities we did together, and I ignored the con side, which itemized our character differences. I loved him and decided that our marriage would surely work. We married when he was twenty-six and I was twenty-two.

45, 46, 47 . . . Three years after our wedding and two years before Jeff, our first child, was born, we started marriage counseling. Like plates shifting, the cracks in our relationship were subtle but significant. We talked less, he worked more, we didn't laugh very often, and our activities together became occasional. In the silences, we started to drift apart from each other. I believed in the value of therapy; Tim didn't. We only went to two or three sessions.

Jeremy was born just twenty months after Jeff's birth, and Tim was spending more and more hours at the office and away from home. Even when he was home, his physical presence was overpowered by his emotional absence. I recognized this behavior all too well. I had seen Tim's father, a self-made and successful entrepreneur, routinely work more than a hundred hours a week. He missed dinners, arrived late for special occasions, and forgot family events. This was Tim's role model, and I tried desperately to reach him before family patterns became ensconced. I pleaded with him to be more present and to participate in our lives, the life of the family we had created. I tried softer methods, too, like baking his favorite coconut cream pie and making comforting dinners of stuffed chicken and mashed potatoes. There were nights when he'd promise to be home by seven, so I'd keep dinner on hold so we could eat as a family, but he'd come home later and later, rarely calling to tell me he'd be late. The boys and I would eventually eat together; they needed to go to bed to be ready for school the next day. I'd wrap Tim's dinner in cellophane and put it in the microwave until he returned, often as late as ten or eleven p.m. The final time we golfed together, we didn't talk for the first nine holes; not one word. As we teed off for our second nine, I complained about the silence. Tim nodded in agreement. Our most lively conversation was about an impending storm coming up the East Coast.

52, 53, 54 . . . The years of silence and loneliness took their toll on our marriage. Tim wasn't interested in talking with a therapist, so I went again, alone, in an effort to save our relationship and family. However, our problems were not confined to just the two of us. Jeff, who was in eighth grade, had started getting into trouble with smoking cigarettes, smoking pot, and drinking.

I remember one incident with clarity. It happened after our traditional Thanksgiving visit to Tim's family's home in Pennsylvania. After the holiday, Jeremy and I returned to Maryland and Jeff stayed on with Tim to hunt deer, a male family tradition. Although Jeff hated to hunt, hated the cold, hated sitting in a deer stand, waiting, I encouraged him to stay. I thought the time with his dad could be a bonding experience, a time when Tim and Jeff would talk, communicate, really share.

The evening after the second day of hunting, Jeff telephoned me. "Mom, I hate it here." He ended a long complaint with the words, "And I'm going to kill myself."

What?! Fighting back the urge to scream with fear, anger, and shock, my mind and heart strained to connect, much like two train cars that jump the track and need to be attached again to be able to function. Jeff had never mentioned suicide before, and I wasn't sure whether he said this for attention, for spite at having to stay behind to hunt, or as a cry for help. I had learned from a school psychologist that if a child has a plan, if a child has really thought out the process of how to kill himself or herself, then there is an immediate and real concern.

"And how will you kill yourself, Jeff?"

"Dad's in the shower, and his car keys are on the mantel in the family room. The hunting guns and ammunition are in the car. I'll take the keys and get a gun and shoot myself." His voice sounded shaky but sincere.

"I'm asking you to wait, Jeff. You haven't even seen Jeremy or me to say good-bye. You need to wait." My mind raced as I struggled to know what to say.

"You just want me to wait. You just don't want me to kill myself. I know." I could hear his head spinning.

Ten minutes after I hung up with Jeff, I called back to talk with Tim. He refused to discuss the situation while he sat in his parents' kitchen. He was adamant; he would talk with me when he came home. My head was in a whirlwind and I didn't know what to do. I called Dr. Derbyshire, the psychologist whom I had been seeing for over a year, and he advised, "Your son is crying out for help; he's suffering. Do not take this lightly."

When Jeff and Tim arrived home, Tim explained to me that Jeff had stolen two cartons of cigarettes from the grocery store his grandfather owned. When I confronted Jeff with this information, he wept with remorse. He felt overwhelmed with problems and, in his fourteen-year-old mind, suicide was his answer.

Tim and I needed to come together strongly for Jeff, so I asked Tim to speak with Dr. Derbyshire on the phone. Tim agreed, and I left the bedroom so he could talk in privacy. When he hung up, I rushed back into the bedroom, wanting to know all that was said. He picked up the newspaper and started reading, saying nothing to me.

Of course I pressed him; I was anxious to know what the doctor had said. Tim looked at me absently and replied calmly, "He asked me, *Does your son need to kill himself to get your attention?*" Tim stopped there.

"And what did you say?" I pushed again. Tim continued to read silently and, for reasons I've never understood, he never answered me. In the following days, he never talked with Jeff about the incident. What makes a father opt out?

Tim and I were losing each other, just as we were losing Jeff. We were losing Jeremy, too, who needed an intact mother and a strong father. He had neither.

I told Tim that I was considering divorce. He responded with one word: *threats*. He was correct that I didn't want a divorce. I was raised Catholic, attended Catholic schools from first through twelfth grades, and took the boys to Church, where they had received the sacraments of Baptism, Communion, and Confirmation. He was also correct in that I longed for a united family: I wanted to grow old with someone who knew my history, someone who knew me when I was just a girl of seventeen. But life was complicated. I needed a teammate, a partner in raising two boys through all the difficulties and traumas that life deals out. I needed a husband who would put family above work, respond when we were unsafe, show up when we had problems, and be there to help me raise our two sons.

57, 58, 59, then 60 . . . I underlined the numeral 60 twice. Counting just one more beat of time and hearing continued silence, I placed the receiver into the cradle.

I waited for Tim to call back. He never did.

About an hour later, the boys came roistering home, saying they had lost track of time because they had met friends at the library. Jeremy had found the books he needed for his project, and all was well. I never told the boys what had happened. At eleven twenty-five that night, Tim came home. I was in bed, curled onto my left side, facing away from the bedroom door, and pretending to sleep. He took off his clothes in the walk-in closet, showered, and quietly slipped into bed. Tim and I were two separate people living in the same house and spinning in opposite directions. The differences between us broke us open, little by little, year after year.

At the same time, our problems, unfortunately, grew larger. Rumors carry like wildfire, especially in a small, independent school, and I began hearing from other parents that Jeff was using drugs like ketamine, crystal meth, and ecstasy. I didn't want to believe it, but when I watched my son be suspended from school and saw him being arrested, I had to accept the truth of it. Feeling powerless, I swung into action. I did everything I could think of to help Jeff and change the trajectory of his behavior: I dragged him to psychologists, I grounded him, and I didn't let him talk on the phone to friends I considered bad influences. I even thought about relocating to another country, far away from the connections he had made. Because Tim's involvement was so passive and contained, I doubted my own emotional reactions and, in my loneliness and desperation, became defensive. Our family was falling apart, and I dreaded what might yet come at me. Even though I still had a satisfying professional life, I was now forty-four years old, edging toward fifty. I didn't want to live the rest of my life in a marriage like mine, alone and empty. The tension of trying to force Tim to talk with me, of pleading with him to be involved in our sons' lives, and of living a life without hope of change overwhelmed me.

In May 1995, I was at my breaking point. I knew Tim loved us in his own confounding way, but he couldn't and wouldn't show up for our sons, for me, for his family. I threatened to end our marriage unless he would attend joint counseling sessions again. We went to the first few visits as a couple. But he was sorry—he said his work was demanding and he didn't have time for meetings. I was sorry, too. I wasn't strong enough to manage any longer. In October 1995, after twenty-two years of marriage, my threat became reality. As hard as it was to leave the marriage, it was harder to stay. I filed for divorce.

When my father heard my decision, he lectured, "What are you doing?! So you're unhappy. Lots of people are unhappily married. Tim brings home his paycheck. He doesn't drink, gamble, smoke, or beat you. What else do you want? You have half a loaf. Dammit. Be satisfied."

I whispered only two words before I hung up the phone: "I can't."

Jeremy analyzed the situation clearly. "If you and Dad had communicated, it would have been better for us."

Jeff responded differently. "I know why you did what you did, and you should have done it years ago, but it still hurts."

Our family was like four figures of a mobile above a child's crib; we danced and turned alone in our stories, but we were all connected, and the tossing and turning of one affected us all. Tim and I had two sons who needed us, and our family problems demanded a full-court press, our total unity. Tim and I weren't that team. We were silent to each other.

After our separation, I thought life would get easier, but I was wrong. Even though one area of tension and stress had lifted, other problems remained, and new ones surfaced. My troubled son Jeff made the decision to leave Calverton for his senior year and enrolled himself in military school. I was disappointed that he would leave the school where he had been since kindergarten and where I was still Head. It was not until much later that I learned from him that he left in order to remove himself from my supervision and gain greater freedom to live the life he wanted, drugs and all.

With Jeff gone, Jeremy and I fell into a quiet routine at home. I had tall iron security gates installed in the entrances of both our driveways and painted the inside and outside of the house, making things fresh. Jeremy often did his homework at the kitchen table while I prepared dinner. The very act of cooking—stirring a pot of sauce and grating cheese over pasta—were balm to my soul. The rich scents of garlic-and-tomato sauce brought back memories of Nonna, and with them feelings of safety and security. How often had I returned to that kitchen table in Nonna's house—that place of refuge, warmth, and family bonding—for strength and inspiration. I wanted my sons to have that too.

Sunday dinners returned to the Sunday meals of my youth, foods like spaghetti and meatballs, braciola, rosemary chicken and oven-roasted potatoes, or linguine with ricotta. Just as Nonna had taught me, tomato sauce was my specialty: I browned pork steak in olive oil and then added garlic and Contadina tomato paste. Stirring slowly with a long wooden spoon, I felt grateful for the enduring love she showed me. I made Nonna's meatballs just as she did, all the ingredients mixed by hand. I rolled small portions of the sticky mixture between my palms and plopped each ball into the sauce wherever I saw bubbles. Jeremy and I enjoyed dining together, and sometimes we invited his friends to share Sunday dinner with a big platter of spaghetti decorated with sauce and cheese, and—just as Nonna had taught me—always starting at the outside edges.

Preparing foods the Nonna way brought me serenity and joy. The scent of tomato sauce would linger for days, and leftover pasta and meatballs warmed our bellies like nothing else could. Jeff's favorite meal was Nonna's chicken and peppers, while Jeremy's was my mom's roast beef with mashed potatoes. Whenever the boys were sick, Nonna's chicken pastina soup was our Italian medicine.

But foods and customs, work and school, couldn't hold back the tsunami that was engulfing our family. Jeff graduated from military school and was accepted to Boston University where, by his junior year, his drug use escalated to heroin. Tim and I refused to pay tuition until Jeff completed at least six months in a treatment center. Jeremy, who also had chosen to attend BU to be near his brother, was mired down by both the family problems of divorce and addiction.

My troubles weren't going away: my marriage was over, Jeff was addicted, and I knew I had neglected Jeremy's needs for years, failing to give him the kind of support he deserved.

Memories of Nonna affected me deeply. She had been so strong. The troubles that woman had seen, the hurdles she had leaped over; there had been an indomitable strength in her. And I needed that strength. It had to be there, in me, in my genes. I needed to be as strong as her.

Through all the confusion surrounding loss and failure, one thing became crystal clear: I needed to forge my own link to the past. For all my life, Nonna and her world had been like a snow globe that I could hold in my hand, shake, and return to. I needed to find her home in Rotondella because it was time. Nonna would be my inspiration and my guide, as she had always been. Nonna was calling me home. Italy was calling me home.

The Board at my school granted me a three-month sabbatical,

and I made my plans. My flight was scheduled to depart on April 5, 1999, the anniversary of Nonna's 110th birthday.

The morning of the flight, as I was putting the last items into my overseas suitcase and forty minutes before I was to leave the house, I was gripped with a familiar panic. My chest tightened and my heart raced. What was I doing? How could I leave my sons, my home, and my work for three months?

I called Dr. Derbyshire and told him in a rattled voice, "I'm not leaving. I'm a mother. Jeff's in rehab . . . Jer's at college. They need me. And I've never left them before. Especially to go overseas. I've never left the school for three months. This is crazy. I can't go, I just can't."

His tone was firm. "If you don't go, you'll teach your sons to be ruled by fear. Your role model will guide them throughout their lives. Fear cannot win."

"I can't get on the plane. I'm going to vomit."

He replied with six words . . .

"Vomit and get on the plane."

ITALY

Chapter 2: The Refusal

1999

Ferdinando refused. Yes, he had relatives in the South of Italy, but he was born in Florence, lived in Florence, and intended to stay in Florence on this day and every day to come.

He was my cousin, a second cousin through marriage, but I was a stranger to him. He knew nothing about my nonna Carmela, my mother Laura, or me. He and I shared only the same olive complexion and the same uncle Patsy, the Patsy who brought my grandfather Vincenzo home to Nonna the night he was stabbed.

There were three of us, all in our forties, gathered around a table in the elegant Le Rampe restaurant, chosen by Ferdinando for its view of Florence. Below us, the Arno was a black ribbon dividing the city in two. Around us, there was the sound of conversation, the chime of silverware and plates. I was in one of the most beautiful cities in the world, dining with a cousin I'd never met and his ex-girlfriend Ombretta, who had remained his friend.

"Ombretta works in China," Ferdinando laughed as he hacked a smoker's cough, "but she speaks English. It's necessary for her business." Ombretta, it turned out, was employed by a Chinese shoe manufacturer to buy Italian leather and other shoe components.

"Please," I interrupted him again. "Come with me to Rotondella. I don't even speak Italian."

Ferdinando sat next to me, elbows planted on the table's edge with his hands in front of his chin and a cigarette dangling between the first two fingers of his right hand. His steel-gray eyes were focused somewhere over my head. He inhaled deeply on his cigarette and the skin around his lips folded into itself like small pleats in suede gloves. As he exhaled, he said only one word: "No."

No, he wouldn't help me find my roots in the isolated hill town of Rotondella. No, he wouldn't be my travel companion. "Where is this place anyhow?" he scoffed. "I've never heard of it." No, he wouldn't be my translator, adding with a roll of his eyes, "My Italian is no help to you anyhow. They don't even speak Italian there. They speak a dialect, and I am not able to understand one word." He capped his litany of *no*s with one more: "I'm an architect and too busy. No."

While it was true that I had only just met him, he had been alerted about my arrival. My mother had called him from Pittsburgh, asking him to look after me while I was in Italy. She had spoken to him in the only Italian language she knew—the Rotondellese dialect that her parents had spoken—but she felt confident that he had understood enough to say that he would help me. She was immediately comforted and so was I. But Ferdinando was now challenging our assumptions.

Shifting away from him in my chair, I considered two other options: one, I could make the trip alone or two, I could find someone else to go with me. The problem was I didn't know anyone else in Italy except Ombretta, and she had been enlisted by Ferdinando to help with translations during dinner and not to take on the job of tour guide to Rotondella. There had to be a way. I wasn't going to wimp out so early. My voyage had only just begun.

"So," he instructed me, "you talk to Ombretta." He angled his chin toward her and in the same professorial tone, he instructed her, "And, Ombretta, you tell me what she says." With communication settled, he lit another cigarette, took a long drag to fire it up, and looked out the window.

I liked Ombretta immediately. Her pixie-cut blond hair complemented her petite face and her crystal blue eyes were wide and sincere. She seemed steady and sturdy in a *you-can-count-on-me* sort of way. She explained that she had been selecting leather for shoe construction for almost thirty years. Her mother and brother, her only sibling, still lived in the north of Italy near Como, and her dad had died when she was just thirteen. "It was a painful time in my life, but I like that I look like him with his light hair and the same blue eyes, the color of the sky." Her laugh was throaty and musical; her words were honest and self-effacing. "We women are tough on ourselves. I hate my nose; it's a little like a hook, no? I want to fix it but probably never will."

Ferdinando had ordered pasta with wild boar as a first course and, as I twirled my spaghetti onto my fork, I thought about Nonna and all the things she had taught me. I explained to Ombretta, "My *nonni* were both born in Basilicata, in a hill town called Rotondella. Nonno Vincenzo was stabbed by the Mafia, called the Black Hand in Pittsburgh, and he died before I was born. It was my nonna who was my safe harbor when I was sad; she was my home base when I ran away from home. I wish I could explain it better, but she is still with me every day of my life. She couldn't even speak proper English or Italian, but she showed me how to pray, how to cook, and how to protect those I love. Does that make sense?"

"So, this is why you want to go back to your nonna's Rotondella? To find her again in some way? To reconnect with her and all she taught you?"

"Yes. If I can find Rotondella," I heard the emotion in my voice, "I will be more complete somehow, and stronger. I'll know my next steps."

Ombretta translated into Italian for Ferdinando my connection to Nonna and why I felt the need to find Rotondella. His fuzzy eyebrows arched, and he looked kindly at me. He nodded. He smiled. He said no.

Ombretta murmured something in Italian, inched her chair closer to him, and started talking quietly. With language blocking me out of the conversation, I studied her. She looked appealingly stylish in her black leather miniskirt, black tights, and black, over-the-knee boots with four-inch tapered heels—making her five feet and four inches tall—light blue cashmere sweater cinched at the waist with a belt in the same leather as her boots, black Chanel bag, Cartier watch—the classic tank model in gold—and Hermès scarf draped casually around her neck in deep shades of black and gold, with touches of blue that matched her sweater and eyes.

Here I was in my L.L.Bean, wrinkle-free black traveling slacks, Clark's specially designed walking shoes worn with TravelSmith socks, an off-the-rack navy-blue wool blazer from Macy's, and my J. Peterman all-weather black bag that slung over my shoulder distributing the weight evenly across the back, the kind with seven zippered compartments and one specific hidden pocket for passport security. I suspected she saw me as a generic American woman: the sensible kind, with sturdy shoes and raincoat, ready to take on a strange new country. I felt like a frump.

Abruptly, Ombretta pushed her chair back from Ferdinando, and took a long drag on her cigarette, the one stained with pink lipstick that was burning unattended in the ashtray.

"I'm sorry, Lee-bee," she said, pronouncing my name the way Nonna did, "but your cousin won't budge. I told him it is out of the question for you to travel alone." Shaking her head at him disapprovingly, she continued, "You don't know the culture of the South, the problems with transportation, the history of poverty, and the distrust of the people. I told him you are his cousin, and he must go."

She shot Ferdinando a blistering look. He shrugged his shoulders, curled down the corners of his lips, and shook his head with his eyes closed.

This cavalier response sparked her anger, "Listen to me, Ferdy. Mafia could be involved. You heard the story about her nonno. What if something happens to her while she's traveling alone? Zio Patsy and the family will never forgive you. Ferdy, you need to think about the Mafia."

"*Zitta,*" he whispered harshly while shifting his eyes dramatically from side to side. "Walls have ears."

Ombretta's frustration with Ferdinando was electric, but she turned and spoke softly to me. "I'm sorry, Lee-bee, really sorry. I'd help you myself, but I'm leaving soon for China. We're busy designing the winter shoe collection and this is my worst time."

I sighed with disappointment, but I was grateful to Ombretta for understanding my need to find Rotondella. Despite her best efforts to persuade Ferdinando, it was obvious he wasn't going to go. It was equally obvious to me that I was determined to make the trip.

Ferdinando asked for the check and brought the meal to an abrupt end. Ombretta irritably rubbed out her cigarette into the glass base of the ashtray, picked up her Ferragamo umbrella, and announced curtly, "*Basta. Andiamo.*" Enough and let's go. Both the dinner and the conversation were over.

Ombretta led the way out of the restaurant with a quick step. As I followed behind Ferdinando, in my head I heard his laughter ringing with disbelief, *Why do you want to go to Rotondella? There is nothing there. I've never heard of this place. You are crazy.*

Maybe he was right. Maybe I was crazy. Or maybe I had asked too much of him.

Through a light drizzle, we walked in silence to Ferdinando's silver Audi. We drove down the hill and along the road shouldering the Arno. Across Ponte Santa Trinita and through the narrow medieval streets, he stopped his car near the Ponte Vecchio and two blocks away from my hotel, not permitted to drive any closer through the pedestrian-only streets. We said our goodbyes with a cheery *buona notte* and a kiss on both cheeks, making promises to see each other again soon.

Alone, I walked back to the Hotel della Signoria. When I was twenty years old, I had taken a trip to Italy with two friends, but we never made it to Rotondella because it was so remote we couldn't figure out how to get there. I wasn't twenty years old now, and I wasn't going to allow fear to stop me from making my lifelong dream come true. I would go, with or without Ferdinando.

Chapter 3: *Fare una Bella Figura*

The next morning when I awoke I had one goal: to make my way to Cortona, a small hill town not far from Florence, where I had arranged to live during my three-month sabbatical. While I was in the States, a friend recommended Cortona, where she knew a rental agent, a Brit married to an Italian, who could help me find a place to live and also connect me with Italian teachers and travel agents. I happily followed her advice and communicated easily via email with Charles Bennington, who responded immediately to all my requests. From an online selection of living accommodations, I chose a lovely furnished one-bedroom apartment, and Charles registered me for both language and cooking classes. He even offered to meet me at the Cortona train stop, from where he would take me to my new home. Although I would have preferred to go directly to Rotondella, I was without a translator. I needed to study Italian so I could manage the trip alone, learn more about the culture of Southern Italy, and work with a travel agent to make arrangements to reach Rotondella.

I set my alarm for seven thirty a.m. to have plenty of time to prepare for a 10:47 train departure from Santa Maria Novella, the main station in Florence. Lorenzo, the hotel concierge, reserved a cab for a nine thirty a.m. pickup, giving me more than an hour to buy a ticket and get to the platform. Waking two hours in advance, I would have plenty of time to repack my suitcases, bathe, wash my hair, dress, enjoy breakfast with a cappuccino in the hotel dining room, and pay my bill. If I had extra time, I could stroll through the Piazza della Signoria, past the Uffizi, along the Arno River, and maybe even window-shop for jewelry on the Ponte Vecchio.

But life is what happens, as someone wisely put it, when you're making other plans. The shower was unmanageable, alternating between scalding and freezing. When I plugged in my dual-voltage hair dryer, a crack like a lightning bolt ricocheted off the bathroom walls, the room went black, and the screech of the hotel fire alarm filled the air. A putrid, burning odor drifted from my hair dryer.

Grateful that I hadn't been electrocuted, I shook my head in disgust as water dripped down my forehead and into my eyes. Wrapping one towel around my body and another around my wet hair, I trudged into the bedroom, called Lorenzo, and apologized for my mistake.

"Yes, madame. It's not a problem." His voice sounded sympathetic.

Did he have an extra hair dryer?

"No, madame, but I can tell you where you might buy one."

"When will the alarm be turned off? I'm sure I'm disturbing your guests."

"Not to worry, madame. The fire department is on the way. They must first check the system to make sure everything is fine. Different electrical systems can be confusing to travelers from other countries."

I thanked him for his kindness, replaced the receiver onto the cradle with a thud, flopped onto the bed, sank my head into the pillow, curled into the fetal position, and hugged the soggy towel around me. Jet lag, exhaustion, tension, and confusion smashed together with feelings of being overwhelmed and alone. All of a sudden, this trip seemed too much for me.

Filled with misgivings about the plans I had so carefully made in the States, I wondered what I had been thinking. How naïve was I?! Even though I had diligently organized the sabbatical, shopped for special travel items to bring with me—one of which just blew up—and found an apartment for a three-month rental, I had never really considered the total costs associated with travel and accommodations and, more importantly, the difficulties of getting to the place I had come to see. I was totally alone, except for a cousin who refused to help me. I wasn't able to speak the language, didn't know anything about the train system, had no idea how to get to Rotondella, and was trusting that some stranger named Charles would meet me and have an apartment ready for me. If Cortona seemed far away from Florence at 50 miles, Rotondella, which was 550 miles away, might as well have been on the moon. I could hear Ferdinando's words ringing in my ears: *Rotondella! Where is this place anyhow? I've never heard of it. You are crazy.*

I could also hear his words about making *una bella figura.* Before meeting Ombretta for dinner, he took me to an outdoor cafe near the Piazzale Michelangelo with a magnificent view of Florence and the surrounding hills. He was pointing out the sites— Bellosguardo, the Duomo, Palazzo Vecchio, and Santa Croce—when the waiter asked me what I wanted to drink. I smiled and ordered a red wine.

Immediately the corners of Ferdinando's mouth dipped into a frown.

"No. She takes a prosecco. We take two *prosecchi."* With this change, the *cameriere* nodded in agreement, *"Certo, signore. Subito."*

I was stunned. I had ordered as I always did: a glass of wine before a meal.

"Why did you change my order?" I asked defensively.

In his halting English, he explained, "In Italy, you must make a good look, or as we say in Italian, *fare una bella figura.* What does this mean? It means that you must learn to do things correctly, *bella,* our way, if you want to stay here. If not, you do things *brutta,* and you look to others in a not-so-good way."

"All I did was order wine before my meal. What could be wrong with that?"

"Boh, in America there is nothing wrong, but in Italy, you *fare una brutta figura.* Wine in Italy is enjoyed *with* meals; this is our culture, our history. Prosecco is a good choice for an *aperitivo* which is what we are having: a little drink before dinner."

So much had happened in the three days since my arrival in Italy. My journal was filled with new information: *buon giorno* is the correct greeting before three p.m. and *buona sera* is the correct greeting afterward; a kiss on both cheeks, the Italian way, starts with kissing the left cheek first and then moving to the right, but only with friends, otherwise a traditional handshake is appropriate; a cappuccino is considered a morning coffee because it is made with milk and never ordered after eleven a.m., while an espresso is fine any time of the day; grated parmigiano cheese is never served with fish; and pasta is never, ever cut with a knife.

As I lay on the bed at the Hotel della Signoria, I had to confront the obvious fact that I was a stranger here and that I didn't belong. What little confidence I had arrived with was dissipating. This morning—blowing up the hotel's electric system and setting off the fire alarm—only reinforced the steep learning curve looming ahead. My mind whirled with thoughts of making a *brutta* or *bella figura,* living in Cortona, and learning the language.

I felt defeated. I was tempted to give up this whole debacle. I thought how easy it would be to take the taxi to the Florence airport instead of to the train station. But I also thought about Carmela and how, ever since I was a child, I ached to know more about her Rotondella, to find it, and to find my own strength. In my mind, she nagged at me, pushing me forward. I could almost hear her saying, *Yes, you are right that there is so much you do not know, but there is so much you need to know. Don't stop now. You are stronger than this.*

Chapter 4: Cortona

At noon I arrived at the Cortona train station. My mind was racing with anxious thoughts about not knowing the language, concerns about living alone in an Italian town where I was the foreigner, worries about how to get to Rotondella, and praying that my British rental agent would show up and have an apartment ready for me. I thumped my large overseas roller bag down two steps from the train's carriage onto the pavement while a bulky man behind me lifted the smaller one and placed it next to me. Before I could utter grazie, buon giorno, salve, or arrivederci, he marched off, his black quilted coat disappearing into the mass of travelers as they formed one block of humanity bustling down the stairwell.

I searched for an elevator but couldn't find one. Taking a deep breath, I adjusted my seven-zippered bag securely onto my back, grasped the handles of both pieces of luggage, waited until the stairwell was completely empty, and then bumped both roller bags down the steps at the same time. The larger, heavier suitcase toppled down two steps, but luckily, my travel shoes gripped, keeping me steady. I was sure I was making *una brutta figura,* and I was grateful Ferdinando wasn't witnessing this scene.

Dragging the suitcases behind me, I shuffled through the underground passage and discovered yet another two flights of stairs looming in front of me. Twenty-two steps. I thought to ask someone for help, but everyone seemed to be in a hurry, already burdened with bags of their own. And I couldn't ask in Italian. I hoped that Charles would appear, but my guess was that he had picked up other clients and didn't want to get involved lugging suitcases.

Finally on street level, breathing hard and clutching my belongings, my heart sank. I didn't know what Charles looked like and hadn't organized a signal, like a man carrying a yellow umbrella, wearing a straw hat, or holding a newspaper across his chest. I had a phone number, but I didn't have a cell phone that worked in Italy. I had read that newsstands sold phone cards that inserted into public pay phones, so I dragged my bags toward a kiosk marked *edicola*. Even though there was a chill in the air, sweat beaded along my hairline.

"Good afternoon, you must be Libby," came a cheerful voice with a British accent. He bounded lightly toward me and stood with his hands on his hips. Charles, tall and lean, had bright red hair. *Ahh*, I thought to myself, *red hair, especially in Italy, would have been a great way to recognize him.*

"You're Charles? I could have used your help with these bags—they're like lead."

An animated face framed by long, rust-colored sideburns, answered my frustrated question. "Yes, I'm Charles, but I never come early. My back is giving me problems, so I don't carry heavy luggage. That's for visitors to do. Welcome to Cortona."

Rubbing his hands together gleefully, his face creased into a smile. "Let's go, shall we? *Andiamo,* as the Italians say."

He trotted to his car and released the hood of the trunk. Standing next to his white Peugeot, he looked like the Italian flag with his red corduroy slacks and green quilted jacket. "This is crazy," I mumbled to myself. "Ferdinando was right."

"Andiamo," Charles called out. "Let's put those bags into the boot." He helped me with a *one, two, three, lift.* I was grateful for his assistance.

"I'm sorry it's raining. It's a gray and soggy day, but I hope it doesn't dampen your spirits."

As he said this, he pointed up the mountain. Almost two thousand feet above us was an ancient town of light gray and parchment-colored stone houses with clay-red roofs punctuated with church spires and winding streets, all dominated by a cathedral built on the summit. An immense stone wall surrounded the city.

"That's where we're going. That's your new home."

Cortona. It looked like an enchanted kingdom of kings and queens with castles and church domes rising in the distance. At the sight, I felt a rush of excitement and joy. My confidence was returning.

Charles's Peugeot became a roller-coaster adventure as we began our steep drive up the mountain. We sped along, winding back and forth on serpentine roads, as Charles began what seemed like a well-rehearsed lecture: "Of course, you probably already know that Cortona is almost equidistant between Florence and Rome. Cortona is in Tuscany, but the southern portion borders the western part of Umbria." He must have given this introduction to other visitors because he continued without pausing. "Italy has twenty regions. Tuscany and Umbria are only two."

I was staring out of the windows at the scenery of rolling hills, olive trees, vineyards, and lakes in the distance. We whizzed past a church with open doors as it welcomed the faithful. In the garden of a villa, two children jumped from puddle to puddle, while their mother stood in the doorway and motioned to them to come into the house. Realizing I was distracted, he raised his voice a notch. "The vegetation and the terrain are very similar in both regions. Always pay attention to Tuscany's magnificent and stately cypresses, the silver sheen to the olive trees, and the fields bursting with golden sunflowers. Both Tuscany and Umbria produce high-quality wine and olive oil; however, Tuscany boasts Chianti, one of the finest wine regions in the world. Umbria also has excellent vineyards and produces a lovely Vin Santo, a special sweet wine served after dinner."

We were now near the top of the mountain, where Charles entered the city through a portal in the antique wall. "See this huge opening that we're driving through? And notice the massive doors and the wall? In ancient times, the residents closed these doors at night to protect the inhabitants of the city from barbarian tribes and other hostile groups. We have over three kilometers of the antique Etruscan wall still intact. This is just one of several doors that remain. You'll have to discover the others on your own."

Now in the city center, we traveled up and down passages so narrow I was sure we'd scrape the sides of the car. My new home was on Vicolo del Fosso, at the end of a one-way street, where Charles and I had to fold in both side-view mirrors to negotiate the ascent. Pointing toward a Sienna-yellow stucco building, Charles chirped, "That's your home—on the third and top floor." The palazzo, he explained, was over seven hundred years old.

"But that's not really old. Not here," he announced proudly. "Cortona is three thousand years old. Some legends say Dardano of Troy founded it. I'm not sure about that, but I do know that civilization here dates back to about 1000 BC and to the Etruscans, who ruled before the Romans. In fact, we are proud to have a world-renowned Etruscan Museum founded in 1727 with artifacts from the fifth century BC. You'll need to visit."

Charles parked the car in front of the palazzo, opened the car's trunk, and skipped ahead pulling the lighter of the two bags. I tumbled out, trying to see everything at once, while wrestling the oversize bag to the ground. No elevator and up six flights of steps. Charles led the way and explained that Italians call the American first floor the *piano terra,* literally the ground floor. The first floor is "up here," he whispered loudly down the stone-encased stairwell, not wanting to disturb my neighbors. I was too excited to be daunted, so I flung my seven-zippered purse onto my back and heaved the heaviest bag up each step with a clunk.

When I finally got into the apartment, Charles had already opened the two large living room windows, allowing the gray lightness of the day to pour in. The beauty of the red terra-cotta stone floor was like nothing I had ever seen in the States. Twenty feet above me, an antique ceiling constructed of bricks and crossed with four hand-hewn wooden beams filled me with awe. In the corner nearest the door was a bumpy-looking couch covered with an orange throw. An olive-green upholstered armchair was placed nearby and flanked by a floor lamp topped with a tobacco-colored shade. The center of the room was dominated by a large wooden dining table and surrounded by four heavy-looking chairs, while a tall china cabinet filled with dishes and glassware was conveniently placed against the wall. On the far side of the room under the windows was a sideboard with a minuscule television set, a combination radio/tape/disc player, and a black dial telephone that looked as if it was from 1950. But I had a phone and was grateful.

To the right, behind the wall of exposed stone, was the kitchen. A small Italian coffee maker sat on the right front burner of the gas stove. I scanned quickly for an American-style brewer, but I didn't see one. Rain splashed lightly through the open window and, on the windowsill, Charles had placed a deep green basil plant that reminded me of Nonna and her cooking. On the kitchen table was a basket of welcoming goodies: a small glass bottle of Tuscan green olive oil, a box of spaghetti, a chunk of parmigiano cheese wrapped in plastic, a small carton of conserved milk, and a can of Illy coffee. In the refrigerator were two large bottles of water, one still and one sparkling, and a bottle of white wine.

"Thanks for all these things," I sang out gaily.

"It's all part of the job," he paused, adding quickly, "and your rent." He laughed at his own joke. "There's no icemaker in the fridge. I know how you Americans die without your ice. Ice and Coca-Cola, right-ho?" He chuckled again, pleased with his humor. "Italians don't use much ice. If you want it, you'll have to buy those plastic thingies at the *mesticheria*. Ah, I love this word because it's typical Tuscan for a shop with a mixture of utilitarian goods, from shoe polish to brooms, coffee cups to thread. They have just about anything you can think of."

He continued to mutter about the bountiful inventory in the *mesticheria* as he walked toward the long narrow bathroom off the right side of the living area. I noticed his beautifully crafted tan leather shoes. I thought again about the saying *fare una bella figura* because Ferdinando had told me that Italians first notice the quality of a person's shoes and then, for a woman, her handbag. I reminded myself to talk with Ombretta about helping me buy Italian clothes and maybe a beautiful pair of boots.

Charles stopped abruptly, pointing to the washing machine. "You'll notice there's no clothes dryer. Always a shocker for you Americans." Dryers, he explained, were rare in Italy. Electricity was expensive and Italians preferred to air-dry clothes by hanging them either outside in gardens, on lines that extended from under a window, or indoor on a *stendino*. My apartment had both a drying line from the base of the bathroom window extending out and over an interior courtyard, as well as a *stendino*, a folding contraption with eight horizontal and ten vertical bars on which to hang wet clothes. Although I didn't have a clothes dryer, I was relieved to see a hair dryer.

On the opposite side of the bathroom was a bedroom with two single beds pushed together, making one king-size, matching night tables, each with a good reading lamp, and a freestanding, large wooden closet. The apartment was spartan but clean and, more importantly, it was mine.

The best part was the view. I had four large windows that opened onto an expansive and picturesque landscape. I felt as though I could see all of Tuscany, with Lake Trasimeno in the distance.

On his way out the door, Charles pointed to a wicker basket filled with travel brochures and tourist information. "After you get settled, have a look through those materials. You'll find lots about Cortona—restaurant suggestions, bus timetables, and local museum hours. I've already talked with a friend of mine—a local travel agent who speaks fluent English—about your trip south. She's never heard of the place where your grandparents were born, but I'm sure she'll have no trouble arranging everything for you. Just let me know when you're ready to meet her. If you need anything else, give me a ring." He handed me the keys to both the main palazzo door and my apartment, pivoted on his heels, and disappeared down the stairs.

I rushed to the kitchen window and breathed in the clean scent of basil as I watched Charles drive away. I wanted to run into the streets to see all that Cortona offered, but instead I poured myself a large glass of water and decided that it was time to organize my new home.

Chapter 5: Study Italian, bella

Among the many books I had read to prepare for my journey south to Basilicata, there were three specific books that I considered most important: two were written by Ann Cornelisen, and the third by Carlo Levi.

Cornelisen, an American expatriate, published *Torregreca: Life, Death, Miracles* and *Women of the Shadows: A Study of the Wives and Mothers of Southern Italy*, in which she documented, in writing and black-and-white photographs, the conditions in regions near Rotondella in the mid-1950s. She had worked in Lucania, the ancient name for Basilicata, for a private British charitable agency called *Save the Children*. Cornelisen lived in the village of Tricarico, seventy miles from Rotondella. To safeguard the anonymity of the people about whom she wrote, she created the fictitious name Torregreca. She wrote:

> *There are dozens of Torregrecas . . . isolated in its bleak beauty where the people struggle today, as they have for three thousand years, to wrest an existence from the rocks and clay that make up their world.*

Cornelisen resided among the people, learned their dialect, and wrote that she grew to *respect them, admire them, dislike them, and be amused, irritated and enraged. We have laughed together and sometimes cried.*

Before I left the States, I searched out Cornelisen, found her phone number, and called her home in Georgia. As luck would have it, she answered. I didn't want her to hang up on me, an unfamiliar voice, so I hurried to explain who I was, why I had called her, and launched into my deep desire to find Rotondella. We talked for a brief ten minutes during which I heard in her voice a melancholy, a tenderness, about the

South of Italy. I didn't remember all the particulars of our conversation, but I did remember her forceful response to my plans, "You cannot go South alone," she warned. "You don't know the language or the people. You don't know what you're facing. You must not do this." But I had no choice, just as she had had no choice. She had written that she was voluntarily bound to the South. So was I. I was born Italian, with my roots firmly placed in the South.

The third book, published in 1945, was *Christ Stopped at Eboli (Cristo si è fermato a Eboli)*. Carlo Levi, a wealthy Italian doctor and painter, had been exiled to Lucania by the Italian government for his anti-fascist activities. He wrote about the South as a place

> *where the peasant lives out his motionless civilization on barren ground in remote poverty, and in the presence of death. We're not human beings; we're not thought of as men but simply as beasts, beasts of burden, or even less than beasts, mere creatures of the wild. We're not Christians, they say. Christ stopped short of here, at Eboli.*

I stacked the remaining books—a huge, unabridged Italian dictionary, two purse-sized dictionaries, travel guides for various regions throughout Italy, and recreational reading—on the wooden mantel attached to the exposed stone wall. Putting clothes away was next, hanging some, folding and stacking others on the shelves in the wardrobe. As I drifted in and out of the bathroom, filling the cabinet with shampoo, cream rinse, toothbrush, and soaps, I stopped to examine the washing machine. The directions were in Italian. I started a list of things to ask Charles.

I had purposefully decided not to bring my laptop so that I could disconnect from work and concentrate on why I came to Italy. During my sabbatical, a colleague with whom I had worked for years was in charge of the school, and I had total confidence that the students and teachers were in good hands. All I needed was several blank journals and a box of my favorite Uni-ball pens.

I had promised to call Mom and Dad when I arrived safely in Cortona. It was two p.m. in Italy, eight a.m. in the States, so I placed a collect call knowing they would already be awake and ready for the day. Mom answered on the third ring; Dad got on the extension. They were delighted to hear my voice, commiserated with me about my travel problems, and offered to call my sons to give them an update. Dad ended the call saying, "Take care of yourself, dearie. You're our one-and-only daughter."

Next, I called Ferdinando to tell him I had arrived. *"Brava,"* was his short response as he dutifully wrote down my phone number.

My third call was to Ombretta, who answered with a quick and efficient, *"Pronto,"* the Italian hello. I immediately launched into my description of Cortona and my apartment.

"Stop, Lee-bee," she interrupted me. "Stop for a moment."

I was surprised by her insistent tone. I thought I must have been speaking English too quickly, so I slowed down and started once again into my recounting.

"Lee-bee. Stop," she cut in, this time more adamantly. "I have something to tell you."

"OK," I said, waiting for her to speak while looking around the living room at two open suitcases, clothes scattered on the dining room table, my multipocketed purse hanging on a chair, and my glass of water too far away to reach.

"I have decided to go to Rotondella with you." She didn't pause but rushed forward. "I've already called Simona, my travel agent, and she has arranged everything. When I return from China, we'll fly to Foggia since Bari airport is closed due to the Kosovo war, rent a car, and drive to Rotondella. Your cousin won't go with you. You cannot go alone."

I was stunned. Turning to look out the window at the rolling Tuscan landscape surrounding Cortona, I felt a breeze caress my cheek. Nonna. She must have been with me from the beginning of this journey, I thought; she must have been orchestrating things from above. I left the States on the anniversary of her birth. I hadn't known how to find Cortona, but I was here. Rotondella had existed only in my imagination, but it would become a reality. Nonna must have sent a small, strong, blue-eyed, blond-haired Italian woman to help me.

"Ombretta, thank you." My eyes filled with tears. "You have no idea what this means to me." I could almost smell tomato sauce cooking.

I could almost hear Nonna say, *"Buona notte."* I could almost see her glasses fogged over with steam while she drained the bubbling pasta water to make linguine with ricotta, just for me.

"I must hang up the phone now," Ombretta responded. "I leave tomorrow and have much to do."

Then, as if she could feel my emotion through the phone, she said softly, "I know how important this trip is to you. We will find your grandmother's Rotondella and your origins. I promise. You have four weeks to get ready."

Then she paused. "Study Italian, bella."

Chapter 6: Getting Ready for Rotondella

With the reassurance of Ombretta's help, my fears about language and travel began to subside. I felt comforted that she understood my need to find Rotondella, so I redoubled my determination to open my mind and heart to all things Italian. My days in Cortona were filled with studying Italian, cooking in a restaurant kitchen, enjoying luscious meals, strolling the evening *passeggiata,* jogging through the park, hiking in the mountains, writing in my journal, and learning about the customs of Italy.

Coffee was my morning elixir. It took me a few days to master the Bialetti, a contraption consisting of three parts: the bottom section filled with water, the middle filter holding ground coffee, and the top bin, into which the brewed coffee rose, screwed onto the base. Once it was assembled and placed over the gas flame to heat, the delightful smells of coffee soon permeated the apartment. I poured the dark liquid into a hefty mug and added an equal measure of heated milk.

Sitting on the deep windowsill in the kitchen, I crossed my legs and alternated between sipping the brew and tucking its warmth carefully against my belly. I broke off a fat leaf of the basil plant, cracked it in half to smell its freshness, and let my mind wander back to the warmth of Nonna's kitchen and her fragrance when she wrapped her arms around me. The rolling hills of olive orchards, vineyards, and Lake Trasimeno in the distance were bathed in pale green light as the sun's rays burned through the filmy air. I breathed deeply, smelling earth mixed with the aftermath of yesterday's rain.

My first morning, I was bathed and dressed by eight, anxious to start my day. Descending the six flights of stairs, I glided my fingers along the walls to feel the permutations of the antique gray *pietra serena* stone and marveled at the workmanship in this fourteenth-century palazzo. Tugging open the heavy, twelve-foot-tall wooden door, I made a quick right turn onto Via Ghibellina, which led to the main piazza. Cortona was built into the side of the mountain and the slope was so steep that I had to walk bending forward, practically at a forty-five-degree angle. Huge buildings, once homes for rich families and now divided into apartments, lined the street, some with private gardens.

When I reached the main square, my lungs were heaving, but I was delighted to find myself immersed in the hubbub of the Saturday open-air market. Like a giant street fair, Piazza Signorelli and the adjoining streets buzzed with activity. Every available space was jammed with large kiosks, food trucks, and white-canopied tents that sheltered rows of tables. Fashionably dressed men, wearing caps and quilted jackets with scarves looped loosely around their necks, stood in groups and gestured as they talked. Women, many wearing knee-high leather boots and carrying cloth sacks filled with bread and vegetables, gathered together chatting and occasionally yelling at their children, who laughed and played tag around their legs. Busy merchants sold linens, clothes, shoes, household items, and foods. Their booths were already buzzing with people buying or bartering for better prices.

The fruit and vegetable stands were works of art. Heaps of thin-skinned, golden-colored potatoes; five or six varieties of green- and purple-tipped artichokes, some for stuffing, others for eating raw, and still others for frying or steaming; mountains of lettuce and radicchio; delicate bundles of asparagus; heavy bulbs of fennel; dark green spinach; hardy, broad fava beans; thick, knobbly-skinned lemons; oranges in shades from deep ruby to bright yellowish-red; and shiny orbs of pomegranates. I wandered from stand to stand and tried to memorize the Italian words written on cardboard signs, and also the way people asked for what they wanted. I paid particular attention to the booths where large groups of women were buying foods or rummaging through piles of clothes, reasoning they must know the best places to find both bargains and quality. As I listened to people around me bicker about prices, I smiled with fondness as I remembered Nonna arguing with Signor Bruno, a farmer who huckstered his produce on her street. To Nonna, the cost of everything was negotiable.

Unlike the street fairs of my youth, where I smelled grilled hot dogs and cotton candy, the scent of *porchetta* filled the air: a suckling pig roasted with garlic, rosemary, and bay leaves. Butchers expertly wielded long knives as they carved the huge slabs of pork into thin slices and filled submarine-shaped rolls of crusty bread.

When I reached the *porchetta* stand, a bulky man was in front of me. His deep bass voice resonated with the words *senta* and *panino,* and ended with *per favore.* When it was my turn, the young girl behind the cash register—maybe the butcher's daughter—smiled, and her pink, glossy lips sparkled in the sunlight. I repeated exactly the words of the man, *"Senta, un panino con la porchetta, per favore."* She answered with a confident, "OK. That is 5,500 lire, please." Of course I was disappointed that my American accent—and probably my clothes—gave me away as being a foreigner, but my enthusiasm wasn't dampened. The gray-haired butcher nodded to me as he sliced the *porchetta* and stuffed it into the bread until it was bursting. He wrapped the sandwich in white paper and handed it to me over the dead pig's head that decorated the countertop.

By morning's end, I had purchased two potted geraniums for my windowsills, one bundle of fresh pasta, a container of homemade *ragù* made with wild boar, a chunk of crusty Tuscan bread, a bottle of local red wine, and a bouquet of freshly cut daffodils for my dining-room table. Before I descended the hill to my apartment, I climbed the steps of the town hall and sat down to eat my *panino.* I wanted to be part of this Italian scene.

Ombretta's admonition to study Italian loomed large. Four hours each morning, from eight a.m. until noon, I dedicated myself to Italian class. Paola, my teacher, a young woman with perfectly arched eyebrows above chocolate-colored eyes, responded with interest when I explained to her, in English, my need to learn enough Italian to travel south to Rotondella.

"Where is this place?" Paola asked as she pulled out a map since she, like Ferdinando and Ombretta, had never heard of it.

"It is a relief to me," she continued in fluent English, "that your friend is traveling with you, but it is also important that you understand some of what is being said. Your grandparents were born in Italy. You are Italian, and you must learn the language to be self-sufficient." With Rotondella as the goal, she was determined to get me ready. Since there were no other students in the beginning level, she was able to structure lessons just for me.

At the end of week two, Paola discussed the dialects in Italy. She explained that most people in the South could speak Italian as well as dialect. "But be careful," she warned, "if they don't want you or Ombretta to know something, they'll speak in dialect. You won't understand a thing."

This was the second time this issue of dialectical differences came up: first with Ferdinando and now Paola. I asked how dialects were different from classic Italian, and why they were prevalent in the South.

"No, not just in the South," she corrected me as she shook her head adamantly. "We have many dialects all over Italy; in the North, too. You must remember that ancient civilizations found both our climate and geographic location desirable. Our land is rich for growing foods. We are surrounded by water on three sides, making navigation—as well as attack—easy. Many countries tried to control us for thousands of years, even before the Romans. In the South, our lands have been fought over and ruled by Franks, Celts, Spaniards, Greeks, and Arabs, and in the North, Germans, French, and Austrians. Remember that Italy wasn't unified until 1861. All these early influences affected our culture and our language. For instance, not only are there different pronunciations of the same word throughout Italy but we have regional differences in grammar, colloquial expressions, and even vocabulary. But you are lucky to be studying in Tuscany," she continued kindly. "We are recognized as speaking the purest Italian because Dante, who is considered to be the father of the Italian language, was born in Florence."

In addition to dialects, Paola announced that there were formal and informal ways of addressing people. "Pay attention. Italians expect you to address them in a formal way. When introduced, you must ask permission to use the informal form."

This was understandable from my high school French studies, but with so much to learn already, I decided it would be easier for me to concentrate on just the informal form. "In America, we're pretty casual with conversations," I countered. "I think the informal *tu* will work for me."

Paola huffed. "I'm serious. America is a young country. Italy is not. We have over two thousand years of history, and language usage is an important part of our culture. In fact, in all of Italy we have three forms when addressing people: *tu, voi,* and *lei.* When you ask someone's name, you must first use the formal, *Lei come si chiama?* The informal, *Come ti chiami?* is used only with someone younger than you, or when you are among friends. In fact, write down this sentence and memorize it: *Possiamo darci del tu?* This is the polite way to ask if you may use the informal form."

I nodded my head and wrote furiously in my notebook. Paola smiled confidently.

Charles had arranged cooking classes for me two afternoons a week. I soon learned they weren't actual cooking classes. They were free labor in a restaurant kitchen.

The restaurant opened for dinner at seven thirty p.m., and I became part of the crew enlisted to help make whatever was on the daily menu. Because artichokes were in season, we frequently prepared them to be used in risotto. The cook taught me that risotto was ready to serve when it was *come un'onda:* still soft and moving like a wave. "Most Americans cook it too long and it becomes sticky like glue," he elaborated. "Better to stop too soon rather than too late."

Every day we made some kind of pasta by hand, a labor-intensive job of mixing, rolling, filling, and cutting. Flour, salt, water, and eggs magically kneaded together to become dough. We rolled portions into flat, thin sheets and then cut them into long, thick strips called *pappardelle,* shaped them into strings that looked like fat spaghetti called *pici,* or sometimes cut them into trimmed squares that we filled with ricotta and parmesan cheeses, porcini mushrooms, spinach, or, sometimes, mashed potatoes. The delicate bundles became ravioli, tortelli, or tortellini.

After work at the restaurant, I went directly to six o'clock Mass at the Cathedral of Santa Maria, which was built in the eleventh century over the ruin of a pagan Roman temple and, in 1325 AD, consecrated as a Catholic church. A group of elderly women loyally attended weekday Mass; their average age must have been eighty years old.

The women greeted me with smiles and reassuring nods, probably because they were thrilled that a younger person was in church. The oldest grandmother, dressed all in black and missing three front teeth, patted the space on the pew next to her, motioning for me to sit. I was the new one, the American, and I was grateful for her quiet welcome.

In the afternoons, when I didn't have cooking class, I jogged or walked through the park at the end of Via Nazionale, where the paved road gave way to a pebbled one that continued and threaded through woods bordered by tall, deep green cypress trees that reached toward the sky like soldiers standing at attention. Children played on the gym set and swirled around and around on an iron disk as they filled the air with squeals of laughter. Many of the older townspeople took an afternoon *passeggiata,* strolling quietly through the paths, talking with friends, or walking their dogs. Others sat on benches that overlooked the green and gold valley punctuated with olive trees, their leaves sparkling silver in the sunlight.

My favorite spot was under the shady protection of a gigantic oak, where I wrote in my journal while enjoying an unobstructed view of the rolling panorama. One afternoon, a frail older woman, dressed elegantly in a tailored wool coat, walked toward me with the aid of an elaborately carved cane topped with a gold handle. She sat beside me. I looked up from my writing and was greeted with her tender smile.

"*Buona sera,*" she said.

It was after three p.m., so I knew to respond, *"Buona sera, signora."*

Paola's words echoed in my head about the necessity of using the formal form when addressing someone older. My mind whirled at the challenge of executing a well-constructed sentence in Italian. Meanwhile, the old woman examined my face closely and looked deeply into my eyes.

"You are American, no?" she asked in English.

"*Sí,*" I answered in a resigned voice, deciding that even my *buona sera, signora,* must have stung her ear.

She seemed pleased to have captured my American essence so quickly and continued, "I speak a little English. I would like to tell you a story. It is a very important story, and is something I remember well. I tell you this because you are American."

I turned toward her and leaned close, as if to say, *I understand and I promise to listen carefully.*

She raised her right hand near her shoulder and made the same kind of rolling wrist movement that Nonna used to make when there was too much to tell. This simple motion brought Nonna and her stories back to me in a significant way. Here was another nonna with yet another story to tell.

She took a deep breath and passed her tongue over her dry lips, pursing them together. I could smell her faint fragrance of roses. She nodded her head once, as if gathering her courage, or maybe her memories.

"When I was a young wife with a husband and two babies, it was the time of the War, the big one, the second one. Our lives were filled with fear. Food was hard to find and many survived eating only beans, potatoes, and chestnuts. We even made flour from chestnuts. We tried our best, but our children had little to eat. We all suffered."

She took another deep breath while reaching into her purse for a tissue and dabbed delicately at the edges of her nose. The memory was painful for her, and I sat quietly, waiting. Her eyes drifted into the distance as her narrative continued.

"Mothers lost their sons in this war. I lost my husband, who was captured and put into a German concentration camp. He passed away there. I never saw his face again. Many of our old people died. My mother died from infection. Medicine was needed in other places. No one was without problem or heartache.

"But I remember June 1944, when the American boys came here to make us free. They came right here to Cortona. I took my children's hands and we ran to the bottom of the hill, way down there, do you see?"

She pointed downward toward the base of the mountain, her eyes filling with the emotion of remembrance.

"They arrived in tanks. Big tanks. Powerful tanks. When we heard the roar, we ran to them. Your American boys were handsome, all with blue eyes and blond hair like the sun. They were young and brave. They lifted our children, mine, too, onto the big machines. We waved and raised our voices in joy. They had chocolates and candies for our children, cigars and cigarettes for our old men. For the women, we just wept tears that our families were safe. They drove up the hill, into our town they drove. What a picture it was—I cannot tell you. I have not the words. But I can tell you this: Your country saved us, saved my children. We can never thank you enough for what you did for us."

With this, she wound down. She wiped her eyes with the tissue. Her husband had died as a prisoner of war in Germany, far away from her. My father and uncles had fought in World War II, and my dad's oldest brother, Fred, was shot down over Germany and died in a concentration camp. I never heard the men in my family talk about their war years. Today, I understood in a new way what America had done for the world, and for people like this woman and her family.

We sat in silence for what felt like a long time. Without warning, she leaned on her cane and rose to her feet. Bending toward me, she touched my cheek, an intimate gesture, and one that reminded me of Nonna. I wanted to hug her and tell her how sorry I was for her suffering. Instead, I sat silently, looking up at her.

"*Buona sera, carissima,*" she said quietly. "I am an old woman. Forgive me my tears." And she walked slowly away.

Cortona became a place where I learned to take time to appreciate the simple joys of life: an old woman's smile, a translucent moon, wild scarlet poppies dancing in the breeze, a crimson sunset, cheese hanging from a vendor's wagon, creamy *gelato,* men talking importantly in the piazza, stacks of freshly baked bread, laundry hanging outside windows, and the little nonna who read the Epistle at Mass but whose head couldn't be seen over the top of the lectern. Paola taught me as much Italian as my head could hold, the restaurant kitchen crew showed me how to make pasta and risotto, the old women at the church welcomed me as their youngest member, and the nonna with the gold-tipped cane shared her story and her tears. I thought about my nonna and all that she had taught me. When she died, she didn't leave me money or diamonds or furs. What she did leave me was much more valuable: a history, my history.

I was grateful for my four glorious weeks tucked into the warmth of the people in Cortona. I had learned many things, but there was still so much I didn't know. I couldn't have a conversation in Italian and couldn't understand the feelings that were under the words. I felt nauseous every time the phone rang and I had to respond in Italian. The little things tripped me up even more than the big things, like remembering the names of many different types of bread at the *panificio,* trying to ferret out the proper sequence for paying and ordering coffee at the bar, or not looking like a deer in the headlights when someone stopped me on the street and asked for directions. Yes, my blood was Italian, but I wasn't raised in Italy. I didn't know the customs or the rhythms of the day. I felt like an imposter, a fake, an intruder.

Part of me wanted to run away, as I had done most of my life, and to be satisfied with what I had already accomplished. The other part of me knew that now, with Ombretta involved, escape was not a viable option. With Ombretta's help, I might be able to find my grandparents' birth certificates and even relatives with whom I could share stories about my grandmother and learn from them whatever I could about my grandparents. My family history would have a clearer portrait, the missing faces could be identified, and I would learn about my own family's bonds with Rotondella. I wanted to belong. I needed to feel connected to this part of Italy, and to my family's history here.

The only thing that kept me going was Nonna. The secrets in her kitchen were more than food and scent; they were a language of history and wisdom, gleaned from experience. It was the memory of myself, as a child, running up those beloved stairs to her kitchen, not only for its warmth but for the stories they told of who she was and where she'd truly come from. Those memories stayed with me through all my moments of doubt.

PITTSBURGH

Chapter 7: Carmela

1958

I hid my bike behind Nonna's garage so that my mother couldn't see it. Then I climbed the thirteen gray concrete steps to Nonna's porch. I counted them—*one, two, three*—and the number was always the same just as Nonna was always the same. Uncles Tony and Jimmy, Nonna's sons, painted these steps every year with the same slate-gray color. At the top of the steps hung her double-wide wooden swing that my uncles, sweating in the August heat, made sure was level and tightly screwed into the overhang.

Through the screen door, I peered into the kitchen. There she stood in front of the stove, my beloved and steadfast Nonna. Engrossed in her cooking and her solitude, she didn't hear me or, if she did, she didn't move. I breathed in her peace and the scent of tomato sauce. Her glasses had slipped down her nose in the heat of the kitchen, and her cotton housedress, belted at the waist, was protected by her trusty apron, a constant part of her attire in the same way some women always wore pearls.

Pushing down on the handle of the door, I inched it open, but the hinges squealed, giving me away. When she heard the sound, she turned, tilted her head, and squinted her dark eyes at me. She knew why I'd come. She threw open her arms and I ran toward her, my body melting into hers.

"Nonna," I choked out in a whisper, like a breath caught in my throat. I needed to say nothing more. She recognized the familiar sounds of my seven-year-old hurt and confusion, just as she recognized the sound of her own heartbeat. She held me, gently running her fingers through my ponytail. The tears swelled as I buried my head into Nonna's forgiving grandmotherly breasts. The dam in my throat that held back despair broke, and here, with Nonna, I allowed myself to weep, shoulders pulsing up and down as I gasped.

She didn't ask why or what happened; she didn't need to. This wasn't the first time I had run to her after a beating from my mother. She stroked my temple and said softly, as if she were healing a baby bird, *"Zitta, zitta,* Nonnared, stop you cry." The sound of English mixed with her dialect soothed me like a lullaby. She once told me, "I call you *Nonnared* because I want a special word for my grand-a-babies. I add *red* like a little nonna. My nonna say the same word to me." With the tips of her fingers, she lifted my chin upward so she could see into my eyes, "It says, I lov-a you. I lov-a you from t'e top of you head to t'e bottom of you feet."

We had a routine we followed, always the same. In a soft voice, she'd take charge, "You too skinny. I have not-a-t'ing good to eat, *ma* sit down. *Mangia,* Nonnared, *mangia."* She pushed me gently out of her arms and toward the Formica table that she kept covered with a red-and-white oilcloth. I sat in my chair, always the same chair, the one on the side and to the left of the head of the table, where she sat. Nonna began preparing pasta. Her meals were her way of comforting me and immersing me in her love.

Nonna was a painter with foods. First, she spooned sauce onto the bottom of a wide, white, shallow platter, and sprinkled freshly grated parmesan cheese over the sauce. When the pasta was ready—not mushy, not chewy, but the perfect texture—she mounded long, wriggling worms of hot spaghetti onto the plate and tapped them into submission with a fork. Always starting at the outside edges, she gently spooned more sauce over the top as she worked toward the center in an oblong spiral design, like the track of the planets' orbits around the sun. After that, she pinched a portion of cheese between her thumb and first two fingers and, starting at the outside edges again, sprinkled it like a dusting of snow. All the time she was painting with reds and whites, she pursed her lips together and moved them slightly in and out, as if her lips could force the sauce and cheese into the perfect picture of her love.

Lifting the pasta between a fork and a big spoon as easily as a crab pinches its prey in its claws, she filled my smaller white bowl. She always gave me too much. This was her way. *"Mangia,* Nonnared, *mangia,"* she commanded as she lowered herself into her chair at the head of the table. Then, like a *maestra,* she watched me.

I concentrated on the way she had taught me to twirl my fork so the unruly strands of spaghetti stayed together long enough for me to shove them into my mouth. Only after she was satisfied that I was eating well did she settle back into her chair and place her hands in her lap, palms up. "What goes on? Why you cry? Where is your mamma?"

I told her that my mother hit me again, but I didn't need to tell her why. Even when she knew her daughter was wrong, she never said a bad word about family. Nonna simply shook her head. "Your mamma has *un cuore di colomba.* You make her angry. Why you make her angry? Be good, Nonnared, and she won't have to hit you. She just wants that you to be good."

Mom was her only daughter, and the Italian way was *la famiglia.* Don't say a bad word about your family. I didn't believe that my mother had the heart of a dove. I didn't care about my mother.

On most weekends, I slept at Nonna's house. I put my toothbrush, pajamas, and extra clothes into a brown Kroger grocery bag and my parents drove me to Nonna's, leaving me with a warning to be good. I never got into trouble with Nonna; she had time for me. We cooked, played card games, and went to Sunday Mass. On Saturday afternoons, we often strolled to Mrs. Maggiore's, an Italian friend who lived nearby. A tiny woman with a long, thin nose that stood out between her high cheekbones, she had a feathery mustache that tickled my cheeks when she kissed me. I sat quietly and listened as the two women discussed their aches and pains and shared their news. I couldn't understand all of their language, but their hand movements along with the tone of their voices gave me clues.

Nonna touched her ears and told Mrs. Maggiore that she had hardening of the arteries and heard sounds in her head all day long and even when she slept. Mrs. Maggiore *oohed* and *tsked* and shook her head knowingly as she countered with her own woes about the pain of her arthritis. That night, when Nonna and I were alone at home, she asked me to put my ear next to hers. "I want that you hear my sounds, Nonnared. *Whoosh-a-whoosh, shoo-a-shoo-a-shoo.* Why they do this, alla day? *Cheep, cheep, cheep.* T'ese sounds never end. T'ey go forever."

I bent down, placed my ear next to hers, and listened closely. I couldn't hear anything, but I wanted to make her happy, so I said excitedly, "Yes, Nonna! I can hear sounds! I can hear whoosh and whizz."

"Is true? You hear noises?" Her voice rose in disbelief as she tilted her head, her eyes wide. I could tell she knew I was lying by the twist of her lips, but our need to share was more important than the lies we told.

Saturday and Sunday night television favorites were Ed Sullivan and Lawrence Welk. She laughed when Ed Sullivan started with, "Ladies and Gentleman, tonight we have a really big show," because she heard it as *Tonight we have a really big shoe.* Like a young girl, she giggled as Lawrence Welk crooned his signature phrase, "Wunnerful, wunnerful!" and her eyes sparkled when Welk cued his orchestra with, "Ah one, and ah two, and ah" . . . as she began to sway her head to the beat of the music. My nonna loved to see the beautiful young people dancing, and she'd *oye* in delight when the show ended with a cascade of bubbles raining like confetti. She loved music. It blurred the lines between cultures, between monetary levels, and between educational differences of those who could sign their name and those who could not.

Sundays were my favorite day to be with her because we walked together in the early morning to Norwood, our Little Italy, to attend eight a.m. Mass at Mother of Sorrows Church. On the way home from church, we stopped at a tiny neighborhood Italian store to buy ricotta so that Nonna could make linguine with ricotta for lunch. The store belonged to a woman named Alvera and it was situated next to a tunnel, so Nonna called her Alvera-the-tunnel, but it came out as one word, *Alverad'tunnel.* Before we opened the door, Nonna leaned close and whispered to me, "We must be careful wit' *Alverad'tunnel.* She gives us old ricotta from last week. I don't want." Then she raised her right index finger and put it on my lips and said, "You stay *zitta zitta.* I talk. *Capisci?*"

Of course I understood and stood mute. The scene was always the same. She and Alvera argued in Italian, waving their arms and raising their voices at each other. Nonna looked at me and wailed, *"Oye,* t'is-a woman never has a good-a word to say about not-a-t'ing. Always prob-a-lem from her about t'ese kinds of foods. Always prob-a-lem wit' t'is-a kind of deliver-ee." Nonna knew Alvera's ricotta was delivered every Saturday afternoon and Nonna refused to settle for anything but the freshest.

Within a few minutes, Nonna started to walk away with me trailing behind her. When we were almost out the door, Alvera yelled, "OK, Carmé. I have-a som-a-t'ing for you can try." She gave Nonna a spoonful of the ricotta she was keeping in a small refrigerator under the counter, and the smile on Nonna's lips told both Alvera and me that this she would accept. It was a game they played, and I always waited for the punch line, that smile from Nonna that told me she knew she was being played all along.

But that day, while I ate, Nonna told me that she was ready to die. She said that she had had a dream that her husband Vincenzo came to her in her sleep to take her home, but when she lifted her arms and reached out to him, a large hand appeared, its palm facing her, to stop her. She sighed. *"Ma* it's no my time."

"You can't die, Nonna," I blurted out, my mouth full of pasta. "Who will take care of me?"

"Sei pazza." She laughed, "One day you let me go. One day I go home to my hus-a-band. No now. No worry. *Mangia."*

Reassured, I finished my pasta, and our routine continued. She leaned forward in her chair, placed her hands on the edge of the table, and bent herself up. *"Andiamo,"* she said softly.

Nonna shuffled directly through the dining room and into the living room while I put my bowl in the sink. I heard her call me in dialect words, "Lee-bee, *ven'aqquá."* She was waiting for me in front of the brown upholstered couch and, when I lay down and settled into a resting position, she tucked a wool blanket around me, encasing my arms and feet and securing it under my chin. She kissed me softly on both cheeks and made the sign of the cross three times on my forehead while mumbling something in Italian. She wasn't talking to me, it seemed, but to God.

Soon I heard the clatter of plates and knew she was cleaning up after lunch. I lay quietly with my eyes wide open, luxuriating in the safety of her home. The late afternoon light drifted through the thin, white lace curtains that framed the windows and shadowed the room. In front of me and hanging on the wall was a picture of Jesus the Sacred Heart, in which Jesus's heart was engulfed in flames. Nonna had told me not to worry because His heart was on fire with love for me. Behind the frame, she had wedged a palm from Palm Sunday, twisted into the shape of a cross.

Above my head hung a picture of Nonno Vincenzo with my great-grandmother, *Bisnonna* Laura Manfredi, Nonna, and my mom when she was just four years old. I loved this black-and-white image because it proved to me that these people, two of whom had died before I was born, had once been alive. In fact, I still cherish it today because it proved to be a key in the search for my Italian family.

Nonno was dressed handsomely in a three-piece dark suit, with a pocket-watch chain peeking out from the second button of his vest. He was short and stocky, with a thick mustache under his large, straight nose. My *bisnonna,* seated in an elaborately carved wooden chair, dominated the center of the group. She had a severe-looking face with a beaked nose, and her gray hair was braided into a crown on the top of her head. Young Nonna, with her gentle expression and pitch-black eyes, wore a floor-length, pleated black dress with lace sleeves and bodice. In her arms she held my young mother, who was dressed in a long, white embroidered gown.

From my position on the couch, I could also see into Nonna's bedroom, which was brighter, surrounded by windows covered with identical lace curtains, where she had slept alone since the death of her husband, Jim. Nonno's birth name was Vincenzo, but when he came to America, he thought this sounded too Italian, so he chose to be called Jim, which he thought was a good, solid American name. I knew from family stories that Nonno Jim had held an important supervisor's job with the water company in Pittsburgh.

"*Oye,* my Jim is a good man," Nonna had told me, clasping her hands together in front of her chest as if in prayer. "He comes a-first wit'out me to *l'America* and gets a big job in Pitts-a-burg. T'ree years later, in 1915, he sends money and brings me from Rotondella. He builds a house for me. He helps many people, gives t'em jobs, and keeps water on to houses of our *paesani* even when some people tell him to close."

"What do you mean, Nonna? Why would people want to shut off the water to the houses of the Italians?"

Her voice became animated, "In t'ose days, t'ere is *La Mano Nera*, t'e Black Hand. T'ey are not Mafia, *ma* t'ey are lik-a Mafia, only not so strong. T'ey tell all Italian people to pay a *pizzo*—some money—for many t'ings like water in t'e house, take away garbage, papers to drive a car or own a store. Many people are poor and cannot pay not-a-t'ing. My Jim listens to nobody because he always helps people from the old country. When people need water, he keeps t'e water on. I tell-a you, he is such a good man." She became sober and distant, remembering a time long gone. *"Ma* he dies too soon, when he is just a young man."

"But how did he die, Nonna?" I asked.

"A knife in t'e belly." She looked away from me and refused to say more. Several weeks later, I asked Uncle Tony, my godfather and her firstborn son, how his father died. He mumbled some words in Italian that I didn't understand, lifted the pointer finger of his right hand, and put it over his lips. He then placed the same finger on top of my lips, as if to close them, and said sternly, "Don't ask so many questions. There are some things you don't need to know."

When Nonno Jim died, Nonna became head of *la famiglia*. As I thought about Vincenzo, who in America became Jim, I decided he was a hero, someone who protected the poor against the rich, and someone who fought to protect his fellow Italian immigrants, especially those from Rotondella. Nonna declared that he was a good man, and of course I believed her. I felt proud to be his granddaughter.

It was many years later when I learned that my grandfather had been stabbed by a member of the Black Hand. There was an argument during a card game and, as Vincenzo was getting into his truck, a man named Lefty knifed him in the gut. Carmela's niece, Adelina, and her husband, Patsy, lived nearby and brought Vincenzo home. He pulled himself up the thirteen steps to the porch, stumbled through the kitchen, and collapsed onto the dining room floor. The doctor came to the house and patched him up. No one called the police. Tony and Jimmy wanted to go after their father's assailant, but Carmela forbade them to get involved. They were sixteen and eighteen, and she feared for their lives. The powerful Jim the Waterman, age fifty-four, died from cardiac arrest during the night, in his bed, beside Nonna.

Soon I heard the squeal of the water faucet being turned off in the kitchen. Nonna's routine was to come into the living room to check on me. I closed my eyes pretending to sleep, but this time I heard her walk directly into the dining room, where the crackling sound of the wooden chair by the window gave away her position. She liked to look out the window while she prayed, reverently holding her rosary with its smooth, blue crystal beads, making the sign of the cross—up, down, left, right—then kissing the silver crucifix before beginning her devotion in Italian. The Hail Mary became singsong as she repeated it ten times for each decade, *Ave Maria, piena di grazia, il Signore è con te*. Sometimes in the quiet of her prayer, I fell asleep. That day, I listened to the words that I didn't understand and felt secure in the love of Nonna and the flaming heart of Jesus.

The phone blared. The serenity created by Nonna's rhythmic voice was shattered by the invading sound. I glanced out the window where the shadows of the trees were long, and I knew darkness was on its way. Nonna's rubber soles squeaked as she walked into the living room where I lay on the couch. I held my breath and squeezed my eyes tight.

Nonna answered quietly. I heard the *teh-teh* sounds that she made by tapping her tongue against the roof of her mouth. Then some *umms* and, finally, "*Si, capisco.*"

I knew it was my mother. I also knew I could not be saved from my mother's anger. I was sick in my stomach, waiting for the dreaded words, *She is here. Come and get her.* They were the truth, and Nonna never lied.

But this time Nonna raised her voice a bit and said matter-of-factly, "No, Lee-bee is no here. I don't see her all day. *Calma*. She be back. *Basta*—enough." In one moment more that seemed like forever, she hung up the phone with a simple, "Ciao."

I didn't know what I would say to my mother when she found me, but I knew she would be furious. I would, once again, be the recipient of that rage.

Nonna and I sat together outside on her porch swing as she rocked us back and forth. This was our special time, when her work was done; this was also the time she was willing to tell me about her life in Rotondella. I didn't know it then, but through her memories, she was connecting me to Italy, to a different life in a different country, a country that was hers, and, by extension, mine. She was giving me my history.

When I felt her body relax and ease into the swaying of the swing, I started, "Nonna, tell me about when you were a little girl."

"No," she said as she looked across the street at Woodsey's house, where spring daffodils were beginning to bloom. "I tell you t'ese stories many time. I have no good t'ing to say. T'ey are no good stories."

"But I love to hear about when you were young . . . please," I pleaded. She laughed when I said the word young as if young wasn't a word in her vocabulary. She took off her eyeglasses and cleaned the lenses with the hem of her housedress. When she put them back on her nose, she sighed heavily. I leaned onto her shoulder as she began speaking.

My imagination transported me to Rotondella, a village at the top of a mountain in the instep of the boot of Italy, in the region of Basilicata, and the province of Matera. In my head, I heard the church bells of Sant'Antonio ringing the hour.

"*Po-ve-ra.* We have no money for anyt'ing. Our house is lik-a no house you never see: no electric, no heat, no water. We work in the fields: Mamma, my brot'ers, my sisters, all of us. When I have your age, seven years and even more young, I work in t'e fields. We walk down t'e hill. Hours . . . *troppo difficile.* T'e mountain is high and t'e way is steep. In snow, in fog, in rain, and in dark we walk. We leave early morning, maybe four o'clock, when t'e moon is still in the sky. And we come back when dark starts at night. Mamma—she tells us what to do. We listen. T'ere is no choice. We work all day, and after many hours in heat or cold, we children get paid one lira or one piece of bread."

She lifted her left hand near her shoulder and made a rolling wrist motion, her way of saying that there was too much to tell and too much to remember. Then, with her right hand, she rubbed her knee, as if the memory brought back an ache.

"And water. T'ere is no water in our village. Rotondella is on top of t'e mountain and water is far below. Women must walk down t'e mountain to t'e fountain and fill *varril* wit' water. How you say in English—bar-reels? First, we roll a strip of clot' long-a-ways and we make it like-a wheel, round and around. It is called a *corona*, we put on top our heads and lift t'e wood container on top of t'e *corona* and carry the *varril* up t'e hill. Even when I am just young, I try to help. My mamma loves me very much and needs me to be strong, so I carry in my arms small clay jugs full wit' water. . . ."

Her voice trailed off and floated over me as my mental movie continued.

"And t'ere is no school for me. We have only one school t'e *governo* starts wit' only t'e first t'ree grades—one, two, t'ree—but no one person in my family goes. We must all work. I can no write. I can no sign my name, and even today, I make my mark with X." She tugged gently on my ponytail. "T'is is why I say you must-a study hard and learn good and strong. Like your mamma. *Oye*, your mamma is always smart in school. She is always one of t'e best."

"But Mom won't teach me to speak Italian, Nonna. Teach me, please. I want to go to Italy one day, to Rotondella. I need to be able to speak Italian."

"No, I can no teach you. If you speak my Italian, t'ey laugh a you a Roma."

I nestled closer to Nonna, cuddling into her sagging breasts, and thought about her life.

All of a sudden, the air cracked with the sound of a car screeching around the corner. It stopped with a squeal at the curb in front of Nonna's house. I sat on the porch swing, exposed. I didn't need to hear Mom's words to know that I had angered her again. I didn't need to have my hair pulled to understand her wrath. I didn't need to see her raise the wooden spoon high above her head to feel the sting of her emotion.

"I take care, Nonnared," my beloved protector told me. "Go inside. You stay *zitta, zitta.*"

I did as she asked, but we both knew she couldn't protect me from my mother's fury.

Chapter 8: Carmela's Ring

1971

Rotondella, the poor, isolated village of Nonna's birth, had grown so large in my mind that when my parents gave me an early college graduation gift of a trip to Europe, I promised myself that Rotondella would be my goal. My two girlfriends understood my longing, and we made a pact, even before we left the States, that we would find the distant village.

After traveling via rail through several northern European countries, we finally arrived in Rome's crowded Termini train station. We calculated Rotondella to be about 320 miles south, but we were stumped because we couldn't find any trains that went there. We inquired at the Traveler's Help Desk, but the young woman had never heard of Rotondella. After she located it on the map, she insisted that she didn't know how to advise us and, even if she could figure it out, the route would be too difficult, especially for people who didn't speak Italian. With a wave of her hand and a roll of her eyes, she dismissed us.

At our youth hostel, the owner, an American woman originally from Chicago who had married an Italian man, explained, "There is no direct train or bus to Rotondella. Even if you rent a car, it's difficult because many roads in the South have been under construction for years and are a mess. Few people in the South speak English and many, especially the older ones, speak only dialect. Even if you spoke Italian, you wouldn't be able to understand anything. This is your first visit to Italy and you can't fully grasp how things are here, especially in the South. Honestly, I think this trip, for you three and at this time, is foolhardy."

That evening, my friends and I stood in front of the Trevi Fountain, each of us cradling three coins in our palms. We didn't know how to get to Rotondella, didn't have extra money to pay for a rental car, couldn't speak five words of Italian among us, and were returning to the States in ten days. They were tired. The August heat was stifling. They were sorry. I was sorry, too, because I wasn't brave enough to go alone.

We tossed our coins into the fountain. With each of my three coins, I made the same wish: *One day, I wish to return to Italy and find Rotondella.*

My family greeted me at the airport, and I was glad to see them, but I was anxious to see Nonna. The following morning, I drove to her home, parked the car in front of her house, and tucked under my arm the present I had bought for her. I looked at Nonna's yard, where she had already hung sheets to dry in the early morning sun and where we cousins had played as children. I thought about the dandelions she picked and washed for salad. I still remembered her surveying her yard with colander in one hand and knife in the other.

By the time I reached the thirteenth and final concrete step that led to Nonna's kitchen, I already smelled the scents of cooking. I peered through the screen door as I had as a child and saw that nothing had changed. Nonna stood in front of the kitchen table and was hunched over her wooden pastry board that she called *u scanatur,* where I saw a large mound of flour shaped like a volcano. I could guess that she was making *i falaoni,* traditional Rotondellese spinach, potato, and meat pies, formed into half-moon shapes that resembled little crusty cushions. She must be making them today, I thought, to celebrate my coming home.

Just as when I was seven years old, the door's metal handle squealed my arrival. Nonna shifted toward the sound, and when she saw me, she clapped her hands together to knock off the excess flour, swiveled on her heels, and threw open her arms. I put her present on the counter next to the kitchen sink, took two quick steps, and lost myself in her warmth. I was now five feet six inches tall, and she had shrunk to four feet eleven inches. My chin rested on top of her head and I smelled tomato sauce and hair spray. Her body felt softer to me, more fleshy, but her arms still held me tight.

"*Oye,* Nonnared," she sang into my chest. "How I miss-a you." She pulled away, grasped my forearms in her strong hands and examined me from arm's distance.

"How beautiful you are, God bless you: *benedic.*" Benedic was the word Nonna said after every compliment to ward off the *malocchio,* the dreaded evil eye. To protect me further, she reached up to my forehead and made the sign of the cross three times. "I so happy you home," she crooned as she moved her fingers, gently tracing the curve of my cheekbone. "I want to hear all about you time . . . all you fun. You had fun, no?" She hesitated slightly, and I knew this question-pause routine, the one to which she didn't want an answer. "*Ma* you tell me later. Now you sit and eat. I have not-a-t'ing good to eat, *ma mangia,* Nonnared, *mangia.*"

I was never happy like this, even in Italy. Still today, in my mind's eye, I see her as she stirs the pot of *sugo* or stands over *u scanatur,* and my heart fills with joy, and the feeling of safety.

"How long have you been awake and cooking, Nonna?" I asked as I raised the tea towels covering three bowls and breathed deeply the familiar smells of parmesan cheese, olive oil, spinach, potatoes, pork, onions, parsley, and spicy hot peppers. She didn't answer. Normally, she would have already been heating a pot of salted water for pasta or pulling things out of the refrigerator to feed me, but today she was engrossed in making something special for my return. She was bent over the wooden board, lost in her work, mumbling to herself and, as usual, praying.

Opening the door of her white Frigidaire, I found three eggs, a small container of milk, a glass jug of orange juice, a jar of Welch's grape jelly—she no longer made her own—half an onion, a clove of garlic, and an open box of Arm & Hammer baking soda, which minimized odors. She was aging and no longer needed a full refrigerator. After being away from her for three months, I was seeing her more clearly, but I wasn't yet ready to let her go.

As she worked, I watched her closely. Her housedress was the same style; this one was green with yellow flowers, a V-neck with a pressed collar—she still ironed everything, including her sheets and towels—and a belt around her waist. Hose on her legs, laced grandmother shoes on her feet, and her apron wrapped around her body where I could see that she had grown wider and plumper. The skin beneath her chin hung and blended into the folds of her neck and jiggled as she moved, but her upper arm muscles were still firm as she kneaded the floury mixture. Her hands worked expertly by muscle memory, and the wedding ring she never took off was covered with pasty dough.

Nonna and I spent the next five hours rolling, filling, folding, cooking, and cleaning up. She was in charge of baking the falaoni in the upstairs kitchen oven, and I was in charge of baking them in the basement oven. On my third trip down the steps, the musty smell of wine mixed with the scent of dried peppers brought back a visceral memory. *La cantina!* Walking to the corner of the basement, I pushed down on the hand-hewn chunk of wood that swiveled on a nail and, *abracadabra,* the sky-blue door swung open to reveal Nonna's cold cellar. The room was cool but not cold, and although it was now empty—another sign of Nonna's aging—it carried a lingering smell from years of storing sharp and pungent cheeses, jars of her canned tomatoes and eggplant, hot peppers strung from the ceiling to dry, and her homemade wine. When I was a child, Nonna allowed me to accompany her on her daily trips to care for the freshly squeezed grape juice. As if honoring a long-held tradition, she ceremoniously lifted the loose lid from each wooden barrel and gently brushed off the light gray *schiuma* that had bubbled to the surface from the fermentation process, careful not to disturb the purple liquid as it self-boiled underneath. When she was done, she replaced the lid and patted lovingly the sides of the wooden barrels, whispering tenderly in her dialect, *Jim'cedd, M mangs,* each a word of longing for her husband, Jim. When I was a child, I was not allowed to enter this sacred space alone, but that day I stood in the center of the room with my arms out to my sides, threw my head back, and twirled in glad circles.

Uncle Tony's deep, melodic voice boomed down the stairs and interrupted my reverie, "Hey, Lib, where are you? It's almost two o'clock. Everybody will be here soon."

I ran to the bottom of the steps and looked up to see my godfather's smile, thick arms, and barrel chest; he reminded me of my mom who had the same olive complexion and handsome face. His hair was graying, and I could see silver sparkles framing his full cheeks.

"Lib, hey, welcome home! We all want to hear about your trip. You look good and happy—*benedic*. But you're too skinny; why don't you eat?"

Before I could protest, he took charge. Of course he did; he was Nonna's firstborn son. "*Andiamo!* Let's get moving," he sang out with a laugh that enveloped me in joy.

The rest of the afternoon was spent in a house filled with the raucous sounds of a family joined together to eat *i falaoni*. A gallon jug of Nonna's red wine sat on the table, along with bottles of Pittsburgh's Rolling Rock Beer for the adults, and orange, cream soda, and root beer pop for the kids. A cacophony erupted as everyone talked and laughed at the same time, conversations starting up naturally at the kitchen table, on the porch swing, and at the top of the thirteen steps. For me, this crisscross of conversations blended together like the confluence of several small sparkling streams careening into one wondrous riverbed. I knew I was home, back in the heart of my family, and it was where I belonged. That day became one of my most cherished memories of *la famiglia*.

After all three families left—mine, Uncle Tony's, and Uncle Jimmy's—Nonna and I cleaned the kitchen and finally sat down at the table. She lowered herself slowly into her chair. I sat in my usual seat next to her.

"*Oye*, Nonnared, we work hard today. *Ma* everyone is happy, no?" She sighed contentedly.

I agreed. I was happy because I had her all to myself again.

She leaned forward and placed her hands on the table, palms up. I took her hands in mine and caressed them, moving my thumbs gently along the blue-colored veins that showed through her thin skin. These hands had worked hard for her family: These hands had gathered shafts of wheat and lifted her babies; these hands had scrubbed clothes in the watering hole and kneaded bread, and these hands had stroked my cheek and protected me with the sign of the cross traced on my forehead. Nonna had said to me once, "One day you learn to let me go." I swore at that time that I never would. I would keep her with me forever. But now, rubbing her fingers, feeling the life in them, feelings the years of heartache and happiness these hands had experienced, I bit back tears.

"Nonnared," she began, her voice cracking, "I am an old woman and one day soon I go to my husband. You must let me go."

She had said it again. I was confused by this sudden bout of melancholy, and before she could say anything more, I jumped up. "But, Nonna, you didn't open the gift I brought for you." I gathered the present and placed it directly into her open hands.

"*Uffa*, what you do!" she exclaimed, all the while shooting me a reprimanding look out of the corner of her eye. "You must save you money," she lectured me in a serious tone while she squeezed lightly the Venetian wrapping paper of reds and greens on a white background. "You spend too much. You need money for many t'ings—for college. College is dear—I know t'is t'ing."

"I brought this for you from Venice. I hope you'll like it." There was no need, not with her, to defend myself.

She nodded a quick thank-you as she peeled back the tape. Inside were three smaller packages, each wrapped round and round with tissue paper to keep the contents safe.

The first bundle revealed a handblown, emerald-green glass goblet from the island of Murano. Five-inches tall, it was a handcrafted bowl on top of a long, thin gold stem and base. It looked like a little chalice, designed by artisans using eighteen-carat gold and hand-painted with white, red, and yellow flowers. She lifted it into the light and adjusted her glasses so that she could see the particular design.

"*Che bella,*" she whispered, then paused. "*Ma* I can no accept. You must take back. Is too much beautiful for an old woman." She immediately opened the other two tissue paper nests and found matching goblets. She lifted the cups into the stream of sunlight shining through the kitchen window, spreading a kaleidoscope of colors onto the table.

Of course they were too delicate for everyday use and maybe for any use, but she understood beauty. She placed them carefully in a line, lifting each one individually, turning it around and upside down and fingering lovingly the painted garlands of flowers. After she had inspected them thoroughly, she took my hand in hers.

"T'ese are beautiful, Nonnared. To Venice you go. In my life, I go very far nort' a Napoli, *ma* Venice—I don't even know where is. And you carry t'ese all t'e way home for me. You are crazy."

In a quiet voice, she continued, "But t'ey are too beautiful for me. I am old and I die soon. Who will take t'ese from my house when I die? I don't know. You must take and keep t'em where is safe."

She touched her thin gold wedding band, rolling it around and around. Her knuckles were lumpy and misshapen from arthritis and hard work. She rocked her body forward, up and out of the chair, turned toward the kitchen sink, ran water, soaped her hands, and worked up a good lather. The faucet squealed shut and she returned to her chair, easing slowly into the same position as before. Her hands dropped into her lap, one cupped inside the other.

"Nonnared," she started somberly. "I lov-a you from t'e top of you head to t'e bottom of you feet. You know t'is, no? My life—it is hard, Rotondella and *l'America*—two different worlds. God, He is good to me and my family. I pray Jesu everyday t'at He take good care of my family."

I felt immersed in the intensity of her dark eyes. She touched the tip of my nose with her right index finger and smiled fondly. "My mamma has a nose like you—a little nose, a pretty nose just lik-a t'is." Then she traced the outline of my lips with her thumb, moving it back and forth, as if to memorize the shape.

"I love all my grand-a-children. But I want t'at you remember me all t'e days of you life. I want t'at you know I never leave you. I want t'at you know I am always here, waitin-a you."

She placed her left hand on the top of the table, turned it upward toward the ceiling, and opened it. Her wedding ring, the band that she never took off—not in bed, not when she cooked, not in the bath, not ever—was cradled in the soft hollow of her wrinkled palm. It had been on her finger for over sixty years.

"T'is is for you. I want you take it. My husband is a poor man in Rotondella when he give it to me. It is not very dear, but it is real gold. I want t'at you remember me."

She threaded it onto the ring finger of my right hand, held it there for a moment, studying it, and then released my hand from hers. Her ring fit my finger perfectly. I splayed open my hand, staring at the gold circle, the symbol of never-ending love. I rolled it round and round, and the shape of the ring began to lose focus as tears swelled in my eyes.

"No. No cry, and no be sad. *Non essere triste,* Nonnared. *Ti voglio bene.*"

Ti voglio bene; I knew these words. Nonna had taught me that only husbands and wives say *I love you* or *ti amo* to each other. From parent to child, it is *ti voglio bene,* three words that mean *I want the world for you. I want all good things for you. For you, I want only the best.*

"*Basta.* I say enough." Nonna stood up, placed her fingers underneath my chin, and lifted my face. Making the sign of the cross three times on my forehead, she kissed the crown of my head, turned from me, and started out the door to check on her laundry, drying in the sun.

I loved her from the top of her head to the bottom of her feet. She would always be in me. She couldn't read or write, perhaps, but Nonna knew the most important thing: Nonna knew how to love.

I got up from my chair and followed her.

Chapter 9: Laura

2011

While Nonna epitomized unconditional love, strength, and consistency, my mother, Laura, demonstrated none of these. In fact, she closed her life off from me. "You can write about your grandmother, but don't ever write about me. My life is my life, and no one needs to know anything about me. That includes you, missy."

Even as a child, I knew that Nonna loved me and somehow Mom couldn't. I grew up straddling the uneasy space of fearing her and needing her, knowing she wouldn't protect me and wishing she would. We danced in endless conflict. "Your father adored you. You became our battleground."

One of my earliest memories was when I was five years old. I remembered screaming at Mom behind my partially closed bedroom door, "I hate you. I hate you! You're not my real mommy. I'm adopted." She burst into my room, held me by the arm, and hit me wherever her hand met my writhing body. "I *am* your real mother. You're not adopted. Only a real mother would hit you like this. You don't listen! Why don't you listen?!"

That was when my brother pulled her off me. "Let her alone," he said firmly. He was only eight years old, but Mom did as she was told. She never hit him, her son.

When I was seven, she called me in from playing with my friends to go to Kroger. I hated grocery shopping; I hated pushing the cart behind her tan trench coat, the matching Tammy cap perched on her neatly combed hair, and her clutch bag tucked under her arm. I hated shopping, but I had to do as I was told, so I followed her through mounds of apples and oranges on the left, zucchini and carrots on the right. Bored with this routine, I placed my left foot on the bottom rail of the cart, and with my right foot pushed myself lazily, like a scooter, and rumbled past her. "Stop that!" she hissed. What she really meant was, *You're going to be in BIG trouble if you do that again.*

Soups, canned vegetables, and cereal aisles were next. I don't know why, but this time I did it on purpose. As she was placing Cheerios into the cart, I stepped onto the rung with my left foot and pushed with my right, drifting halfway down the aisle and away from her. When I turned around to look at her, her eyes flashed with anger and her right eyebrow raised in that menacing way. Then she did what many Italian mothers did when they had had enough: She raised her right hand, turned her palm downward and parallel to the floor, and bit down on the outside edge of her hand. Then she lowered her hand near her chin and shook it sharply at me, up and down, three times. Her rage zoomed in on me like a bullet. I lowered my eyes in submission and stood frozen in place. She nodded, satisfied that I finally understood. She turned the corner and disappeared.

The aisle was deserted. A clear runway. Not a person in sight. I placed my left foot on the low bar of the cart, then—with all my might—peddled with my right foot. The cart blasted forward. I raised my right foot, planting it next to my left, and hung onto the handlebar. I sailed down the aisle. A breeze caressed my face. The store shelves became a kaleidoscope of color. I was flying through a rainbow. Mom couldn't stop me. I was free. I hung my ponytail behind me, and it danced in the wind. My last vision was of neon lights pasted onto a sterile white ceiling. The last thing I heard was the clanking of cans. The Cheerios box landed on my chest.

My mother pulled me out from under the rubble, abandoned our shopping adventure, dragged me to our Mercury station wagon, and shoved me onto the back seat. When we got home, she whipped off her coat and grabbed the wooden spoon, the long, thick one she used to make tomato sauce. I made a mad dash toward the front door, but she gripped my skinny arm like a vise.

"Why are you so obstinate?" Her voice got the high, screeching sound that made me shiver. "Why? Why are you so defiant?" I yanked away from her just as the wooden spoon caught my right leg. "You need to listen! Why don't you listen?" and with this, the spoon hit its mark: my backside. It stung, but I didn't care. This wasn't the first time she'd hit me, and I knew it wouldn't be the last. I didn't cry. I refused to give her the satisfaction of tears. I didn't even say I was sorry.

I wiggled and wrangled, twisting and turning in every possible direction that my body could move, but I couldn't avoid three more solid cracks: my upper right arm, the side of my head, my right thigh. I was sick of being hit and sick of her. I swiveled as hard as I could, jumped up, then slammed my body down onto the floor and slipped out of her grasp. Digging my knee into the rug and pushing off my back foot, I tried to scramble out of her reach.

She snatched my ponytail. My head jerked back. I swung my arms and legs wildly, desperate as a cat being drowned. We spun around and around. I would not be captured. I would not be hit again. I held on to the base of my ponytail so that I could pull away from her. I was dizzy and my vision swirled. I broke free. Or maybe she released her grip. Whichever it was, I was hurtling through the room like a thrown discus. I saw the air conditioning unit in front of me, the box-shaped window kind that extended six inches from the wall. I knew I was going too fast to miss it. I tried to turn my body. I tried to put out my arms to stop the blow. My face hit first. My right cheek rammed into the edges of the grate and my nose cracked against the raised knob. Pounding noises popped in my ear. My lower body kept going the extra six inches and slammed against the wall, my belly taking the brunt. I fell to the floor.

"Oh my God! It never ends with you!" her voice cried out somewhere behind me. "Now look what you've done!"

And that's when I began running away: out of the house, onto my bicycle, down the alley, and to Nonna, my refuge.

The relationship between my mother and me didn't change much as I grew older. She was unpredictable, and I predictably ran from her.

But it wasn't always bad. When I was in middle and high school, there were times I came home to the comforting scent of simmering tomato sauce or, better yet, Uncle Tony at the kitchen table, where he and Mom laughed, taste-tested hot peppers, and ate thick chunks of parmigiano with crusty Mancini bread. Other days, I entered a dark house, no scents of cooking or even life. Mom would be in bed, with the bedroom curtains closed tight. When I opened her door, she would awaken and yell, "The light! It's too bright. Close the door!" She suffered during those years from Dad's infidelity, his emotional outbursts, and, at times, the rage that he took out on her. Under her psychiatrist's care, she found relief in prescribed medications, some to help her sleep and some to help her wake up. When I was a kid and watched cartoons in the living room, she would stumble through the room, stepping over me as I lay on the floor, mumbling, "Don't talk to me or even look at me until I've had at least four cups of coffee." I hated her doctor and didn't know what to do.

At some point, I don't remember when, she substituted her doctor's prescriptions with religion. Always a devout Catholic, she found refuge in God and her faith. She attended retreats, enrolled in and led Bible studies, and became a powerful prayer warrior. During those years, our relationship modulated and would momentarily soften and change. She was quick to beseech God on my behalf, and I was quick to ask her to pray for me. There were days when she could be strong for me, but it never lasted. Her fragile emotions would boomerang back with force and ugliness, but usually only with me. Even into adulthood, when I had children of my own, I couldn't trust this juxtaposition that was my mother, her seesaw of emotions and mixed messages.

In 2004, when I was fifty-three years old, four major events collided in my life: I was diagnosed with breast cancer and had a bilateral mastectomy; Dad, the person who after Nonna was the most significant force in my life, died; Jeff, my firstborn son, became addicted to heroin, with track marks in his arms and legs and abscesses on his feet as he continued to bounce in and out of halfway houses, detoxes, and treatment centers; and I left the school community where I had been Head of School for seventeen years.

With so much loss, I felt adrift and ached for stability and safety. There was no need for me to continue to live in Maryland. Jeremy had graduated from college and had accepted a job in Florida. Jeff was continuing his chase up and down the East Coast for his next high. He was clear about himself: "I'm going to do what I'm going to do whether you're in the United States or not." I considered relocating to Pittsburgh because Mom was now eighty-three and widowed. She and I looked at several homes in Sewickley where we could each have our own independent living areas, but in the end she decided that it was best for her to continue to stay at the Masonic Village Retirement Community, where she was safely tucked into her routine.

In September 2004, in an effort to find some safe ground after all that had happened, I decided to move to Florence to heal and find peace in my deeply rooted memories of Nonna. I wasn't sure how long I would stay, so Ombretta and Ferdinando found a short-term rental apartment for me and had offered to meet me at the airport. Their arms were open, and I accepted their help with relief and gratitude.

I considered living in Rotondella, but it was breast cancer that held the trump card in my decision-making. Florence is 200 miles from Milan, where Dr. Umberto Veronesi, an internationally renowned researcher and surgeon, was pioneering significant advances in the treatment of breast cancer. If I had problems with a recurrence of cancer or my surgeries, I wanted to be close to Milan and the resources of Dr. Veronesi. My cousins in Basilicata would have embraced me with love and helped me in every way possible, but the distance from Rotondella to Milan is 620 miles and requires an eleven-hour drive. I knew that if I lived in Florence, Ferdinando and Ombretta would *take care* of me if a problem arose, especially with my health. It's the Italian way—*la famiglia*.

Life in Florence offered me distance from my problems and a chance to reflect on all that had happened. My sons and Mom seemed fine with my physical absence because I stayed close via phone calls. After spending three months abroad, I made the decision to make Florence my home away from home. I returned to the States, put all my belongings in storage, packed several suitcases, and made my way back to Florence.

Over the years that followed, Jeff and Jeremy visited me often, and Florence became a second home for them too. I traveled several times each year from Italy to the States. I spent the majority of my time with my sons, but I made a deliberate effort to travel as often as possible to Pittsburgh to be with Mom, maybe out of obligation or maybe out of wanting a connection, probably out of both. Every August and December as well as most Mays found me at my mother's door, longing to be with her, but always unsure how I would be greeted.

Often, her eyes would fill with gentleness and comfort, and she'd croon, "I'm glad you're in Italy. Sure, I miss you, but I'm happy that you're happy." But, more often, her words drove us apart as wide as the ocean that already divided us. Some comments were mildly critical: "What did you do to your hair this time?" Other comments cut deeper wounds: "What would I do without your brothers? Their wives are more like daughters to me than you are. They cook for me and take me to my doctors while you're traipsing around Italy."

"I'm not traipsing around Italy. I'm in Florence, writing. I'm writing about my family's life with addiction. Maybe our story will help other people who are suffering."

"Writing? You don't even know how to write."

In the shifting tides of my mother's approval and disapproval, I struggled to believe I knew what I was doing. My joy at being in Italy told me that I was in a good place and doing the right thing, but I also felt guilty for not being at her side as she aged. She was right that my brothers and their wives had to pick up the slack, and I was grateful. When I first came to Italy for my sabbatical in 1999, I was a drowning woman and Italy was my life raft. In 2004, it had now become my safe place, my home.

In March 2011, for Mom's ninetieth birthday, I flew from Florence into Pittsburgh to be with her. I arrived at her apartment jet-lagged and bedraggled, and our time together went downhill from there. The confrontations began almost immediately. For months before her birthday, she had told me, "I want nothing for my birthday. Nothing! Do you hear me? I don't even want to acknowledge that I'm ninety years old." But the social director at her retirement village had told me that many residents enjoyed receiving cards in lieu of a celebration.

Excited about this idea, I sent out a mass email asking friends to send her birthday cards to honor her special day. Over 250 cards arrived.

"I *told* you to do NOTHING," she raged. "You're my nemesis."

"I'm so sorry. Please forgive me. I was only trying to do something kind. I know you told me you didn't want anything for your birthday, and I know I should have listened, but they are just cards."

"Listen, missy. This is a travesty. You don't need to ask forgiveness. You need to eat crow. You need to get down on your knees and grovel."

Later that day, my older brother asked me, "Why do you keep coming home and putting your head into the mouth of the lion?"

But eight months later, I wasn't prepared for what would happen when my younger brother's phone call brought me from Florence to Pittsburgh and to my mother's hospital bed.

For most of her long life, Laura was an Italian beauty with a voluptuous figure and slender waist, but now her body, small and frail, eighty-seven pounds, looked gray and spent, like a used match tossed into the white sheets. Suffering from an infected intestinal blockage, she was scheduled for surgery. She feared death and had prepared for it: Father Dave had heard her last Confession and given her the Catholic sacrament of Last Rites.

As I stood next to her bed while we waited for the final call for surgery, Mom reached up and touched my hand. Her skin felt soft and cold as she caressed my palm as if she were stroking a baby bird. "I need to tell you something, but please don't hold it against me after I die."

I dreaded whatever she might tell me. I shifted my weight from one leg to the other and listened to the whir of the intravenous infusion machine to my left and the muted conversation of nurses in the hallway. The smell of acrid antiseptic stung my nostrils. In the distance, the church bells of Sewickley's Saint James chimed the hour.

"I've wanted to tell you something for a long time." Her expression serious, she breathed in the stale air of the room and, on exhale, she said in a clear voice, "When you were a child, I never loved you."

I never loved you.

These words hung in the air between us, almost as if I could reach out and touch them. My heart pounded. Like the pressure of holding my breath underwater, my throat constricted and I couldn't speak. Even though I had known these words were true my whole life, I never imagined hearing them spoken aloud—especially not so openly. I could understand how a mother might not *like* a child, but love is something I thought was born into a woman, somehow baked into the marrow that gives life to bone.

"It's not my fault that I didn't love you." She enunciated each word sharply, as if she were poking me through the air. "I didn't know how to love a daughter. My mother never knew what to do with me. Italian immigrants wanted a firstborn son. I was firstborn, but a girl. I was a disappointment, a failure to her. All my life I was a failure to her. I didn't know how to love you because I never felt a mother's love."

This deflection of blame didn't surprise me. Of course it was Nonna's fault, or mine, or someone else's, certainly not her's. But she was dying; maybe not during this upcoming surgery, but the end would come as surely as the Pittsburgh snowfalls would turn to slush and clog the city streets.

Her voice, gentle this time, wedged into my thoughts. "I wish I had loved you more, taken care of you. I've lived all my life with this regret. I'm sorry I never loved you. My life was hard. I suffered."

This I understood. I remembered Dad hitting her, her hitting him back, and the policeman coming to the house to take him away. She recanted, he came home, and they were happy. Until it started all over again.

"I don't even remember you as a child. I'm so sorry. You were a gift, full of love and fight, but I never appreciated you. It was only a few months ago that I realized how much I love you. One morning when I was in deep prayer, I felt an overwhelming maternal love for you. I never felt that way before. The Lord put it on my heart, and I realized how much I love you. I love you now, more than ever. Can you understand?"

Could I understand? I wanted to, but her words *I don't even remember you as a child* hit hard. I remembered housekeepers better than I remembered Mom. Dad and Mom had started a portrait photography business, working together, building it from the ground up on a little money and a lot of guts and grit. Ted was a self-made and hardcore entrepreneur, driven to be successful at all costs; his personality was big and bold, and he had a relentless vision for what they would achieve. Laura was the cautious one, the worrier. She was razor-sharp, a whiz with numbers, and she kept track of profits and losses—and, in the early years, there were many more losses than there were profits. Torn between the business and home, she was spread impossibly thin. I wanted to say, *I don't remember you very well either, Mom. And sadly, I mostly remember the bad parts.* I wanted to say that, but I didn't.

The nurse entered the room. It was time.

Bending down, I kissed her forehead, warm against my lips. I paused within inches and examined her face. Her flawless complexion was achieved, she proudly told the nurses, by applying olive oil after waking each morning, her personal elixir against aging. I wanted to memorize the shape of her high cheekbones and her full lips, the lower one plumper than the upper, just like mine. Her eyes drank me in, and I felt my life's history rush by, like one gigantic cold gust of wind across the back of my neck.

"Do you realize how much courage it takes for me to tell you this? Please forgive me."

She didn't die, not that day.

Chapter 10: Laura Remembers

2012

Mom recovered from her surgery, but she never fully recovered her strength. In September, nine months after her bedside confession, she was in another bed, this time in a nursing home under hospice care, attached twenty-four hours a day to a cannula connected to an oxygen canister. Her body was shutting down: congestive heart failure was the official diagnosis. Pneumonia had set in, and the doctor said her lungs would continue to fill with fluid because her heart wasn't strong enough to repair the damage. Neither our kindly Dr. O'Donnell nor the hospice nurse knew when the end would come: maybe in six months, maybe in six weeks.

Mom had been failing for several years: three broken hips—one of them she broke twice—and two gut surgeries. In my mind, she straddled the space between fragile and invincible, and this juxtaposition was complicating for me. Just when I feared she was down for the count, she'd sprint ahead, reviving like a cat with nine lives. Her mind was always sharp, and she remembered phone numbers better than anyone I ever knew.

"Mancini Bakery?" I asked.

She hadn't called the number in over twenty years. "Oh," she pursed her lips together, thinking, her black eyes flashing, "it's . . ." She gave me the number. I called and she was right.

I admired her and admitted, easily and with a sense of pride, that she was smarter than I was and, in fact, that I thought she was the smartest of all our family. She read three newspapers daily—the *Wall Street Journal,* the *Pittsburgh Post-Gazette,* and the *Pittsburgh Tribune*—completing the crossword puzzles and jumbles. All this at ninety-one years of age. Mentally agile, emotionally fragile.

I returned from Italy to take primary responsibility for Mom's care. While I was in Pittsburgh, I stayed in her apartment, located in the independent living portion of the Masonic Village complex, the retirement community where both Mom and Dad lived and where I slept in the guest room. I was comfortable there and could walk between her apartment and the nursing home.

My typical daily schedule was to visit with her from nine o'clock in the morning until after she had lunch, leave for several hours to run errands, swim, or rest, and then return again at five o'clock to help her with dinner, staying until bedtime at nine. In our time together, she supervised me as I straightened her room and organized the clothes in her drawers and closet. When she felt up to it, she got out of bed for a little exercise. Sometimes she allowed me to read to her, but most often I sat in a chair next to her bed and we talked. In our quiet moments, she asked me to lie next to her. She was tiny and had lost even more weight; now she weighed only seventy-eight pounds, so there was plenty of room in the single bed for the two of us. We lay side by side, held hands—my right and her left—and stared at the ceiling.

One October morning, when the autumn sun streamed in and warmed her room, I asked her, "Is there anything you want to talk about, Mom? Anything you want? Anything you need?"

"No. Is there anything you need? Are you hungry?" she asked innocently, always concerned if I was eating properly. A typical Italian mother.

"I'm fine, but I have a question. One I've wanted to ask for years," I said solemnly. When Dad had died eight years earlier, I was left with questions, and I didn't want that to happen again. The signs of death's approach were clear: her legs were swelling, her energy diminishing, and she slept a little longer during each afternoon. I knew there was little time left to ask anything of her.

Her thumb moved gently back and forth, as if outlining my bony knuckles. She was smart and she must have felt the gravity of the upcoming question because she said nothing. I waited for her to give me permission, but when it didn't come, I plowed forward.

"Mom, why did you beat me?"

She might have been ready for the question, or maybe she simply wasn't surprised because she answered quickly and without hesitation. "You were bad," she told the ceiling, answering in a light, matter-of-fact voice, as if the answer were obvious. "You never listened to me."

"But you didn't hit the boys. Only me. Why did you hit only me?" I asked, my voice growing sharp.

"The boys listened. You never did. All my life I tried to break you, but it was impossible."

Her answer came at me like a slap; I could almost feel the sting. I bolted into a sitting position, erect, sharply attuned to her words and facial expression.

"So it's my fault I was beaten?! Mom, I was five years old, seven years old, ten years old. Are you saying it was my fault?"

Feistiness. Mom's fiery and quick temper reared its head, rose up, and struck out. Her eyes flashing with heat, she arched high her right eyebrow in that malevolent way she did when I was a child, and countered, "If you had listened to me, young lady, I wouldn't have had to hit you."

Shocked at her unrelenting righteousness, my eyes glared with disbelief and my heart ached for the hurt and confusion of my childhood.

"What an irresponsible answer," I practically yelled at her—*practically* because even in my discomfort I was aware that people were in the hall, there were nurses nearby.

"It was my fault? It's just that easy for you to dismiss your bad behavior?" I stood abruptly, picked up my purse, and, in an effort to cloak the rage that was boiling inside me, I lowered my voice and said, "I have nothing more to say to you. But I can't accept this."

Without another word, I stormed out of her hospice room, leaving my mother alone, a ninety-one-year-old woman stuck in bed, connected to an oxygen tank, too weak to get up on her own. As I hurried down the hall and away from her room, I heard her voice pleading, "Libby, please come back. Don't leave me. Please . . ." A nurse's voice came from behind me: "Libby, your mom is calling you."

"Yes, I hear her," I said quietly as I continued down the hall, never looking back.

At five o'clock that evening, Mom rang my mobile phone. "You always return to me about now to help me with dinner. I just wanted to tell you that you don't have to come back tonight. I know you're upset."

"I have no intention of coming back tonight."

It's true I had many conflicted feelings about Mom, but it's also true I dreaded her death. That night, my dreams played out this strife.

I dreamed I was in bed crying and Tim came into the bedroom with a book, a Harlequin novel that he had found on the desk. He thought Jeff and Jeremy were reading a "dirty" book. He started showing it to me; it had a pink cover. Finally, I said, "I'm crying, can't you see? My mom died. I'm alone. I have no mother." He was apologetic, smiled, and continued talking about the book.

In the second segment, I was at an airport and my luggage was missing. I wanted to call Mom to tell her about my problem, but my cell phone wasn't working. Desperate, I grabbed another person's phone, but it was made of paper—yellow stickies that I had to put in order and press. The number was something with sevens. It was folly, so I threw the paper phone to the ground and ran into an office, where Jeff and Jeremy were sitting at a big mahogany desk covered with phones. I told them I needed a phone, and they said I could use one. I had to get in touch with Mom.

In the last segment, I was sitting in our family dining room, looking out the window at Mom and Dad. They were having dinner outside on a wooden terrace and there were other diners, too. He was holding her hand, smiling, and looking lovingly at her. He was handsome—tall, slate-gray hair—and she was beautiful in a soft, flowing, knee-length dress, belted at the waist, her hair styled in her normal way, but the color was darker. I was thinking how beautiful and happy they were. She moved like a dancer, and he was proud to be with her. In the dream, I knew she had died, and I didn't want the dream to end. I awakened in tears.

*

The next morning, I entered her room in a quieter, more subdued state. Although I was still hurt and angry, I had written about my dreams in my journal, recorded my feelings, and reeled in my emotions, as if they were a wild fish thrashing on a line. Mom was dying, and I needed to hear her answers.

"I'm glad you're here," she said with a warm and welcoming smile. "I missed you." She patted an empty space on the bed, next to her hip. "Sit down next to me." I did as I was told.

"I know you're upset with your brothers, but don't be," she said sweetly. "It's not healthy." She patted my wrist as if to soothe me.

Confused by such an absurd statement, I blurted out, "With my brothers? What do they have to do with this? I'm not angry with them. I'm furious with you!"

"Me?! Why are you angry with me?"

"Mom, this isn't going to work," I responded quietly, my voice modulated, my eyes soft. "You pretending not to understand is too painful for me. It isn't good for either of us and has to end. You and I both know you beat me when I was a child, and when I grew too big to beat, you whipped me with your words. Let me be clear: I'm leaving again and I don't know when I'll be back, but I can't stay and play this charade."

As I stood to leave, I heard her sigh as if in defeat, or maybe in resignation.

"Please don't run away from me. Not now. Not again. Just give me a minute. Lie down next to me. Please."

I was conflicted. She was right that I wanted to run from the room and from her, as I had done all my life. Running away was my default mode, just as feistiness was hers, but this time I hesitated because my need to know was greater than my need to run. I had to take this chance to learn the answer to my question, one I had harbored in my subconscious for years. I took a deep breath and lay down next to her. Her body was warm, but her hands were icy cold. I wrapped both my hands around her left hand and tried to warm it.

"What do you remember?" she asked quietly.

"You ask me what I remember. Do you really want to know?"

In my peripheral vision, I could see her head nod slowly up and down. On the pillow we shared, I felt her slight movement.

"I remember a lot. I remember when I was five years old and you beat me because I told you I was adopted. You burst into my room, lunged at me, hit me to the floor, telling me only a real mother would hit her child as you hit me. I remember when I was six and we got into some harangue upstairs. You tried to grab me, but I dodged you and ran down the steps, intent on escaping out the front door. You screamed to my brother, 'Stop her,' and what was he supposed to do? He grabbed me. In my mind's eye, I can still see his face, contorted with regret and sadness as he held me. When you got to me, you grabbed my ponytail and threw me onto the floor, kicked me. I remember when I was ten and we were both in the kitchen. You were at the stove cooking something and I was sitting at the counter. I must have sassed you because you slapped me so hard I lost my balance and tumbled onto the floor. The stool tipped over, crashed onto my belly, and I cried out in pain. You just walked away. The windows were open, and our next-door neighbor must have heard me screaming because she walked across the yard and knocked on our front door. You refused to answer and told me to do it. I smiled and reassured her that everything was OK by telling her that I had fallen in the kitchen—just a careless accident—and I was fine. When she walked away, you were waiting for me. You said something like, 'You never cry. You always smile in front of others,' and you beat me again, but this time I took your punishing blows in silence. I remember the last time you hit me. I was fourteen and we were at the kitchen sink. I'm sure I gave you some kind of smart-aleck response because you flung your arm back and whacked my face so hard that I fell onto the linoleum floor. While I was on my knees, I thought, *"What am I doing here? I'm bigger than she is."* I got up, leaned toward you, looked you squarely in your eyes, and said, 'If you ever hit me again, I'll hit you back.' You never hit me again, but you beat me with your words."

Silence. The room reverberated in silence. Rays of sunlight flickered onto the white-plastered ceiling. The oxygen tank whirred. The air smelled sweet from the potpourri I had placed next to her bed. She had clasped my hand tighter and tighter as I retold my memories.

"You remember all that?"

"That and more."

She breathed deeply, and I could almost hear her thinking. Finally, after all these years, I had told her my truths and recounted a few of my memories. Maybe the telling was the most important part for me and was good enough. Maybe she didn't need to respond.

"It's true. It's all true," she said slowly and deliberately. Her grip on my hand released like the lid of a pressure cooker.

It's true. It's all true. When she said those words, my heart felt like it was splitting open and releasing the dam of long-held hurts. I could almost feel the ugliness, resentment, and pain, all those emotions that I had lugged around for years, finally gush away from me.

"I've prayed for years that you would forget all that had happened. I've prayed for years that the Lord would erase all those memories." I sat up in bed and looked at her. Tears filled her eyes, but she held them back. She didn't break away from my gaze.

"All my life I've had a hole in my heart. Now I realize the hole was you. For years, I've prayed that the Lord would let me die. But He has kept me alive. Maybe He has been keeping me alive for you. You don't know your mother, not the real me. I've never let you know me. This needs to change before I die."

She raised my hand to her lips and kissed it. For the first time in my life, I felt my mother's tears.

Chapter 11: Laura's Secrets: Mafia, *Malocchio*, and the Missing Year

In the days that followed, an animated Mom regaled me with stories of her past, until she grew tired, closed her eyes, and drifted to sleep. I listened intently and recorded each detail in my journal. My mother didn't object. She often told me, "Get your journal and write this down." She was the puzzle piece that connected our three generations of women: Nonna, Mom, and me. In the end, I was to learn how Rotondella, like a giant mother spider, wove a web that freed Nonna and grounded me but suffocated and smothered Mom.

"I've kept secrets my entire life," Mom began. "It's no one's business what happened to me. Except maybe now it is your business, so that you can understand who I am and why I was the kind of mother I was."

Her earliest memory traced back to when she was a child and concerned the Black Hand, the locally organized extortion subgroup of the Mafia. They issued threats and fed on fear and violence throughout Pittsburgh and its suburbs.

"The *Mano Nero* entered my consciousness when I was just three or four years old. You might think that I was too young to remember, but I remember clearly.

"Late one afternoon," she continued, "when the sky was dark and threatening rain, my grandmother Laura, my mother, and I were in the kitchen. I was playing on the floor with pots and pans when I saw two men dressed in black walk from the alley and toward the back door. My mother glared at my grandmother and gave a sharp nod toward the hallway. The tension in the room ricocheted through me. Nonna Laura scooped me off the floor, whisked me upstairs, and hid with me in the back of a bedroom closet, behind the suits and dresses.

She kept one arm around my waist and one hand clamped over my mouth. The men's footsteps tromped—boom, boom, boom—up the stairs, through the house, and eventually into the bedroom where we were hiding. One of the men opened the closet door. Nonna Laura tightened her grasp around my body and mouth, but the man never moved the clothes. After some time, the kitchen door banged and they left."

This performance, my mother explained, was a way to threaten her father, Vincenzo. The men acted as though they would kidnap Laura, her dad's only child. Vincenzo, whom people called Jim the Waterman, was a big deal in town, with a powerful position as a supervisor at the water company. His approval and connections were priceless because he could give men jobs. Not only that, but he also controlled the water flow to homes throughout Pittsburgh. When Italian immigrants didn't pay their *pizzo*—extortion money—to the Black Hand, Vincenzo was ordered to turn off the water to the delinquent homes until payment was made. But he wouldn't allow people, especially his Rotondellesi *paesani*, who had already paid their water bills, to be intimidated. He refused to enact the tyranny of the Black Hand.

Mom was reluctant—or maybe afraid—to elaborate on this episode, even in response to my questions: *Who were these men? Why would Italians prey upon their own countrymen?* In her silence, she reminded me of Nonna when I had asked why Vincenzo was stabbed. Because of Mom's stubborn refusal to say more, I employed my own research skills and found articles about the Black Hand in the *New York Times,* the *Pittsburgh Post-Gazette,* and the *Chicago Tribune.* I learned that members of the Black Hand were loan sharks and blackmailers, gamblers who ran numbers, and small-time gangsters who shook down business owners for money. The *Pittsburgh Post-Gazette* reported that between 1926 and 1933—Mom was born in 1921—there were more than two hundred gangland killings in the Pittsburgh area. The McKees Rocks Historical Society published a picture taken in March 1930 of Al Capone when he visited the Rocks. There were legendary stories about Capone being flush with cash, handing out hundred-dollar bills to children, waitresses, and friends.

Gathering firsthand information from family and friends who had grown up during those years, I learned that members of the Black Hand waited at the end of the McKees Rocks Bridge on payday and demanded a cut of the men's wages from the P&LE railroad yards. The story of the Fourth of July Massacre was particularly savage, when under the cover of fireworks and in the parking lot of the Villetta Barrea Club in Norwood, members of the Black Hand shot those who had defied them, leaving pools of blood in the open field to be found the morning after. The five Rizzo brothers were stonemasons who refused to pay the required *pizzo,* so the Black Hand threw bombs at their family's front porch while the brothers, stationed at their front windows, shot bullets at the passing car. Rocco Gentile double-crossed the Black Hand and was found dead in a gutter in Cleveland. When Uncle Jimmy was a kid and coming out of the Stowe Township Parkway movie theater, he witnessed three men dressed in black brutally punch and kick a man until he could no longer move and lay helpless in the middle of the street. One of the men turned to the onlookers and threatened, "You didn't see anything. Understand? Or you're next."

I also heard concerning stories about Nonno Vincenzo. He often invited men, again dressed in black, to sit at his Sunday dining table, eat, drink grappa, and talk, while Carmela cooked the familiar foods of Rotondella. On Thanksgiving Day, he stood in the garage in front of his Ford Model T Touring car, one of the first in town, and handed out turkeys. The men kissed his hand.

During the Depression, Vincenzo provided seemingly unlimited money, food, and abundant coal. Once a week, men in black delivered foodstuffs to their basement. Each Friday, Carmela ordered Laura to go to a friend's house, but instead Mom hid behind the garage and watched as Italian women from Norwood queued in front of the door and held wide their empty sacks while Carmela distributed rice, flour, cornmeal for *polenta,* potatoes, chicken, pork, or whatever the men had brought. Before leaving, the women kissed Carmela's hand.

These facts about the Black Hand combined with what I had learned about Jim the Waterman raised concerns and even more questions in my mind. Although this information proved nothing concrete about Mom's father and his compliance and/or cooperation with the Black Hand, it did seem to implicate him. When I reported these facts to Mom and pushed to know more, she was loathe to talk about it. Frustrated by my insistence, she flared, "I don't know what to tell you. All I know is that money was my father's calling card. I'm not sure what all he did, but we lacked for nothing."

These stories both intrigued and confused me: intrigued me because they were fascinating, cloak-and-dagger stories of outlaws and renegades, but also confused me because Nonna had staunchly claimed that Vincenzo was a good man, a man of integrity. Obviously, he couldn't have been a thug, a gangster, or a member of the Black Hand, and he surely wouldn't have had dealings with those kinds of men. I badgered Mom for more information, but she didn't want to talk about her father. It was only later that I guessed why.

Mom had one overriding desire: to talk about her mother. "The problem with me telling you about my mother," she moaned, "is that you loved her and she loved you—grandmother to grandchild. It's the same way I feel about your sons. I adore them. But for my mother and me—mother to daughter—it wasn't like that. All my life I was a disappointment to her. Even as a little girl, I knew I was nothing to her. Nothing."

That her own daughter could be *nothing* to Carmela didn't jibe with my tender feelings about my beloved Nonna. Laura, however, harbored different memories.

"It started early. When I was just a child, my mother squirreled away enough money to force Vincenzo to bring her mother, Laura, from Rotondella to Pittsburgh. Using his connections, my dad could make things happen. When mom's mother, Laura Manfredi, arrived, Carmela was ecstatic. Of course, Nonna Laura, after whom I was named, moved in with us. My mom was devoted to her mother, and I remember how happy she was. The two of them, mother and daughter, talked for hours, gossiped about everyone they knew, including my father. They totally ignored me. In time, I became a thorn in their sides, and my grandmother shunned me. I hated her. I could understand dialect, so, in order to get back at her, I told my father everything they said.

"By the time I was five, my mother shooed me out of the house each morning, 'Go and wait on Mr. Montesanto's steps. When he comes home from work, he'll give you a present.' I waited, sometimes all day, yearning for and expecting a gift. When Mr. Montesanto came home, I would rush up and, with expectant eyes, ask for my gift.

"He'd hem and haw and say, 'A gift? Sure, but I forgot it at work.'

"Day after day, I waited on his steps. If I didn't, my mother beat me for not obeying her. Sometimes, I'd sneak away and hide in the tall grass in a nearby field with the hope that she would worry and search for me. She never did.

"When I was six years old, while my Nonna Laura was holding my infant brother Jimmy in her arms, she died. I was happy she was gone. I thought my mother would turn to me, talk with me, and spend long days with me. It never happened. She never showed me any maternal love. Never."

This loss must have wounded my mother deeply because she told this same story four or five times. This deep rejection, so early in her life, laid the groundwork for problems yet to come.

In the middle of Mom's first-grade year, Vincenzo moved his family from their Italian neighborhood in Norwood, where the high school had so many students from immigrant families that it was nicknamed Rotondella High, to a new, three-story brick home that he had had built on a large corner lot in Stowe Township, an Anglo-Saxon Protestant community. Carmela hated being ripped from her Rotondellesi community, where the people shared the same dialect, foods, and religious traditions and beliefs. Vincenzo allowed Laura to finish first grade in Norwood, but the next year she had to go to a new school near their new home, where she didn't know anyone.

"On my first day of school, my mother made me wear a blue party dress with red socks. She wanted others to know that even if we were immigrants, we had money and we belonged. When I got to school, the kids laughed at me. I wept. I wanted to be like all the other girls, and I was smart enough to know that my family was different.

"When the children heard my name, Laura, an uncommon name during those years, they mocked me. The other girls had names like Helen, Margaret, or Anne. I cried to my father, and he came to school and demanded that they call me Mary. My legal name is Laura Maria, so the school complied. Even though his English wasn't very good and even though schools were frightening institutions to immigrants who couldn't read or write, he talked with the principal and took care of me. My mother couldn't have done this. Language divides people, and my mother's stubbornness in continuing to speak dialect did just that. As soon as she opened her mouth, we were tagged as immigrants, and illiterate.

"As I grew older, I refused to speak dialect. I studied hard, read intensely, and learned as much vocabulary as possible. I prided myself on my language skills. This hurt my mother and cut an even deeper rift between us."

Most of Mom's painful remembrances emanated from the disconnect between cultures, between the old country of Rotondella and the new country of Pittsburgh. My mother was caught between two worlds with vastly different norms, expectations, and histories. Although these stories were painful for Mom to remember, I hung on every word because they gave me insight into my beloved Carmela's life, her life before I knew her. Fascinated by the tales of the old country, I had an insatiable curiosity about the superstitions, foods, and culture, but Mom would not be my guide. As much as I longed to be a part of, and to connect with, our Italian heritage, Mom wanted nothing to do with it. She blocked my passage, declaring, "I rebelled against everything Rotondella. I was sick of it. I refused to live life according to rules from a time and a country that wasn't mine."

But even in her rebellion, she begrudgingly, in fits and starts, recounted some details about the evil eye, called the *affascn* in dialect, a concept that she abhorred. Her meager explanations were unsatisfying, so once again I began my own research. The *malocchio*, I learned, meant evil spell, curse, or hex. The evil eye was cast by a glare of desire or jealousy, and the person afflicted suffered some malady, usually a headache or a stomachache. Nonna was a *sfascinatrice*—from the Latin *fascinum*, meaning witchcraft—who had learned from her own mother how to banish the evil eye. The procedure was based on ritual, myth, and deep religious beliefs. Carmela performed the rite as she had been taught. She sprinkled salt in the shape of the cross into a shallow bowl of clean water while saying prayers—Our Father, Hail Mary, and Glory Be—each three times. Then she touched the blessed water and made the sign of the cross three times on the forehead, hands, and heart of the afflicted person, while again repeating the prayers. If she yawned, that was a sign that the evil was leaving the person, coming through her, and banished. When Carmela was finished, Laura was told to dump the water outside where two roads intersected, thereby making a cross.

"This humiliated me," Mom rolled her eyes in disgust, "especially when my girlfriends visited, and women from Norwood wove their way down the hill and into the house crying out, *'Oye, cumma Carmé,* I have the *affascn.*' When I was thirteen, I was supposed to learn this practice from my mother, but only in church during Mass and ten minutes immediately before midnight on Christmas Eve or Easter. My mother called this deeply religious ritual *ric a cap* in dialect, but I also heard it called *battesimo* or *dicendo la testa*. But when the time came for my mother to teach me, I refused."

Her rebellion didn't end with the evil eye. There was also the cultural tradition of matchmaking. Nonna and her friends called it *mashiat,* but in Rotondellese dialect the word is *matrimonije cumbnat,* or in Italian *matrimonio cambinato*. Immigrant parents were authorized to choose the person their child should marry. Uncle Jimmy laughed when he told me that Carmela and Vincenzo had committed both Laura and his older brother Tony to pre-arranged marriages. "Those two were stuck. Neither of them wound up marrying the person Mom and Pops chose, and this caused lots of problems at home. By the time I was born, they had forgotten about me and had made no match. I got lucky." He also told me about a thirteen-year-old girl from Norwood whose parents told her they were taking her to get shoes but instead took her to church to get a husband.

One particularly quiet day, as Mom and I lay side by side in bed, she became somber and distant. Maybe it was because we weren't looking at each other, or because of our physical closeness, or because my journal was out of reach, but for whatever reason, her tone of voice—subdued, almost furtive—signaled that she was about to share something important.

She grew melancholy.

"By the time I was in eighth grade, school was a lonely place," Mom began faintly. "I was embarrassed to bring friends home and I felt isolated. My girlfriends came, but only once. My father touched them on their shoulders and backs, and he looked at them in a way I knew wasn't right. My mother saw it, too, but she didn't say anything. When she had to leave the house, she always asked one of her friends to stay with me.

"She knew I adored my father. When I was a child, he loved and protected me. He was my hero. But my father worship ended when I was in ninth grade.

"My dad was in the garage and late for dinner. This was an anomaly: When pasta was ready in an Italian home, you ate. I offered to go to the garage to get him, but my mother told me to let him alone because he was busy. I ignored her and started out the door. She grabbed my arm. We started to push and pull until she explained that my dad needed to be alone because he was in the garage giving himself a treatment for venereal disease.

"When I heard those words, *venereal disease,* I went catatonic. I fell unconscious onto the floor. Mom was forced to call the doctor to come to our home. I was sick for a long time. From that moment on, I hated my dad. I refused to sit with him at the dinner table. My parents couldn't do anything with me. I was trapped in a house where my mother never showed me any affection and I couldn't live with the man who was my father. My reality became clear and my spirit broke.

"I missed my entire ninth-grade year. The teachers sent my assignments home, and the next year I returned to the tenth grade, where I continued with my classmates. I had completed all my work alone, while living in a house with parents who were practically illiterate."

Her words hung in the air. She was depleted. Neither of us said anything more about this, not that day. However, that night, while I recorded the day's events in my journal, I wondered why she decided to tell me about this now, after keeping it a secret for decades. There was little time left to ask questions, so the next morning, while I sat next to her, I wove our way back to the previous day's story.

"You missed an entire year of school because you learned your father had VD. An entire year! How is that possible?"

"It's just the fact of the matter." She kept her voice restrained, but her eyes glared at me. "You have to understand. I loved him; he was everything to me. This news broke me. Something inside me broke. I don't remember what happened next, but they told me that I went catatonic and fell onto the floor. I can't explain it any better."

"I can understand that you were disillusioned, brokenhearted," I said softly. "And I'm sure you were ill and catatonic, but a year, Mom? That has to be an exaggeration."

"It's not an exaggeration. It's the truth. Aren't you proud of me that I graduated with my class? And that I earned a full scholarship to college?" she countered in an agitated voice. "I did all that work alone. I had to ask others for help—neighbors and friends—especially with the math, because it was difficult. My parents couldn't help me with anything. Do you see how strong I was? How self-reliant I was? How determined I was?"

"Yes, Mom, of course I do. You're smart. You've always been smart. When I was a kid, you could carry on a lucid telephone conversation, calculate the totals of money orders on the adding machine, and still have part of your brain left over to yell at me."

We laughed, each lost in our own thoughts. The voices of people passing in the hallway and the steady hum of the oxygen tank filled the air. I had pushed hard enough and was resigned to let this thing go. But it was Mom who began again.

"You can't believe I missed an entire year of school because I was sick, but it's true. I don't know what else to tell you."

I looked deeply into her eyes, the eyes I had known all my life, dark like Pittsburgh coal.

She paused and sighed.

Next, almost in a whisper, she said, "You think I was pregnant, don't you?"

I nodded my head, yes.

"If I was, I don't remember."

My mother had either erased the memory or blocked it out; whatever had happened, she had buried the pain deep inside, in a place she couldn't seem to reach. Had her father abused her? I didn't ask. It felt heartless to push her to go back in time and relive what had happened seventy-seven years ago when she was a fourteen-year-old child. My mother was dying. She didn't need to be interrogated by me. What she needed was compassion—and that I could give her. I nodded my head in solidarity and understanding. Then, I let it go.

ROTONDELLA

Chapter 12: Thelma and Louise

1999

On May 7, Ombretta and I boarded the inaugural flight of Federico Secondo Airlines, the only nonstop flight from Florence to Foggia. There were only five passengers on the plane, including us. When we landed and entered the arrivals terminal, all the information signs were written in Italian and no one spoke English. I was able to read just a few signs, but people spoke Italian so quickly that I couldn't understand anything. I was disappointed. I had purposefully taken classes in Cortona with the hope of learning enough Italian to work *with* Ombretta, as a teammate. In Tuscany, I could speak English and get by, but here that wasn't the case. I quickly realized I would have to depend on Ombretta completely from now on.

My petite leader stepped up immediately. After we retrieved our checked weekender roller bags, she shepherded me through car rental with my American passport and driver's license. She also chose the appropriate insurance coverage, including theft, because, she explained, car theft was not unusual in the South. From Foggia, we would drive three hours to Rotondella.

We loaded our luggage into our rental car, a 1998 Alfa Romeo convertible. I was comfortable driving a manual transmission and she was comfortable giving directions. On her lap she held a thick manila folder bursting with maps, confirmations, hotel phone numbers, and a copy of the photo that had hung above the couch in Nonna's house. Even Ferdinando had contributed by making a hand-drawn map of my family tree.

We were Thelma and Louise: two women united on an adventure. I was Thelma in this duo, the one who needed help, while

Ombretta was Louise, the organized and meticulous one who took charge of the trip even before we left Florence. Not only had she supervised flights and car rental but she had already attempted to find my relatives by scanning the phone book and calling several homes in the Rotondella area that had listed last names of Perciante or LaGuardia.

"Don't worry, Lee-bee," Ombretta assured me while sitting comfortably in the passenger seat and lighting up another cigarette. "I'm not surprised that I couldn't find any family connections by calling homes. People were probably suspicious when my call came out of the blue and they heard my questions about their names. I'm sure that once we get to Rotondella things will fall into place." Her blue eyes flashed with intelligence and good, old-fashioned know-how. We whizzed down the highway, going the posted speed limit of seventy-five miles an hour. I felt like I was speeding, even though every other car zoomed past us, leaving us in their dust. This served as yet another reminder: I was the foreigner.

Basilicata's stony and arid landscape contrasted starkly with Tuscany's fertile rolling and gentle hills. The Apennines, in the South of Italy, are barren, rugged mountains of sedimentary rock that dip and rise in quick succession like waves crashing into one another. As we drove, their gray crests descended into low-lying valleys where spring green foliage heralded the bloom of May's early warmth.

What did Ombretta know of Basilicata? I asked and was surprised by her scholarly response: "This region was originally called Lucania, from the Latin word *lucus*, meaning forest. The Greeks established control somewhere around the eighth century BC. From the third century BC, the Romans colonized the land and cut down the trees for shipping and building needs. In time, they destroyed the forests. After the fall of the Roman Empire, other groups invaded the area. For instance, the Saracen pirates, who were Arabs who terrorized the Italians living near the water, raided the plains. People were forced to move inland and to the safety of the mountains."

I was stunned that she knew so much. When she saw my surprised look, she answered flatly, "Lee-bee, I am not so smart as you might think. All Italian students learn these things about our country, just like, I'm sure, you learn about the United States. This is our country's history."

What did I know about this land of my grandparents? I knew that ever since I was a child, I loved the way the word *Ro-ton-del-la* rolled off my tongue. Before making this trip, I had done some research and learned that Rotondella towered two thousand feet above the Ionian Sea, where earlier generations built Rtunn, as it was called in dialect, at the highest possible point. In fact, Rotondella was called *il balcone dello Ionio,* the balcony of the Ionian.

"The biggest problems were water and diseases," Ombretta continued. "Because of the closeness to the sea, the people suffered from epidemics of malaria and typhoid. The higher locations helped keep them safe from the mosquitoes in low-lying areas and along the water's edge."

"So, is this why," I questioned, "Rotondella is up so high and why Nonna had to walk down the hill to fetch fresh water from the fountain or the river's edge? In Carlo Levi's book, *Christ Stopped at Eboli,* I read about the horrible living conditions in the South, and how many people died of disease and poor medical care."

Yes, she nodded. "This is the history of the South, what we call the *Mezzogiorno,* and some of the major reasons why many people left to go to America." She took a long drag on her cigarette, signaling the end of the conversation. In the comfortable quiet that ensued, I realized that Ombretta and I were becoming friends.

Ombretta's voice broke the silence. "We've been driving for more than three hours. We must be getting close. Pay attention." As we rounded yet another curve, she tilted her head and peered out the window. Checking the map with the hand that wasn't holding a cigarette, she pointed to a location. "I think that's it," she offered. "I don't see a sign yet, but I'm pretty sure that's your Rotondella. Turn right here and we'll go up the mountain."

Within ten minutes, I saw a sign that I never imagined I'd see: *Rotondella, 5 kilometers.* I had hoped for this day for more than forty years. Pulling onto the side of the road under the sign, I leaned my chin against the steering wheel and focused on every letter to remember this moment forever. Neither Ombretta nor I spoke.

At this solemn juncture of my life, where the past rose up to meet my present, I thought about Nonna: how she refused to teach me Italian—"No, I can no teach you. If you speak my Italian, t'ey laugh a you a Roma"—and how she reluctantly answered my questions about her hard labor in the fields, and when she told me how she had longed to travel to the sea that was too distant for her to reach.

Ombretta leaned forward, touched my arm, and said softly, "It's OK to cry." Like Nonna giving me permission to feel my sadness, I allowed myself to weep.

After several minutes, I blew my nose and wiped my face, put the car in gear, and continued up the hill. There we found another sign: *BENVENUTI a Rotondella*. I felt excitement and anticipation as I looked at Ombretta, whose bright smile mirrored mine.

Looping up the mountain and navigating the serpentine road of curve after curve, we drove higher and higher. As we neared the top, we took a sharp left-hand turn and passed a few homes on the right, with a view of the sea on the left. We were close! Following the narrow, steep road, we finally crested into Rotondella's main square, Piazza della Repubblica.

My eyes couldn't take in everything quickly enough. The buildings were old and worn, in colors of slate gray, clay red, and rosemary purple, all built like a wedding cake in horizontal layers, as if they were stacked on top of one another. At the top of the mountain there stood a church as their holy protection. Totally engrossed in what I was seeing and not paying attention to where I was parking, I drifted the car into a curb, jerked my foot off the clutch, and the engine burped and sputtered off. I took a breath and turned to Ombretta to apologize, but her voice cut me off. "Lee-bee, don't move. Look out your window."

Seven men had already circled our car. Arms crossed in front of their chests or hands shoved into pockets, they were inspecting us with guarded expressions, much like soldiers who were sent out to protect their village against intruders. Many of them looked like Nonno Vincenzo in the photo: the same piercing, coal-black eyes; the same dark hair; the same short, stocky body. Dressed in dark quilted winter jackets and wool caps, eyebrows arched in suspicion, they were waiting for us to announce ourselves, declare our mission.

I threw open my car door and leaped into action like a horse at the starting gate. In a strong voice, I announced, *I am Perciante. I am LaGuardia.* Slowly and tentatively, a few men responded affirmatively: *Sono Perciante, Sono LaGuardia.* More men appeared, walking toward our car, and their voices added to the chorus. Perciantes and LaGuardias were everywhere! Surely I had found family. Some of these men among the crowd had to be my cousins. I turned toward all the men who answered as being Perciante or LaGuardia and began kissing them on both cheeks, asking, *"Cugino?"* I was praying that just one person would answer yes.

Just as I was bending toward another man to give him a kiss on the cheek, I heard Ombretta's shrill voice calling my name. She grabbed my arm, pulled me back with one word, *basta!* She whispered, "You must stop kissing everyone. They are not your cousins." She told me that in many Southern Italian towns like this one, the villages are filled with people who share the same last name, much like in the States, where there might be many Browns or Smiths who were not related. "You must stop," she commanded, her gaze intense. "You're not in America. You're in Italy. This is not our way."

Turning away from her, I scanned the group where, just moments earlier, the men had been responding happily to me. Now, their attitude had changed. They had heard Ombretta's scolding voice. Maybe they had at first thought we were two Americans, lost and uncertain. Now they realized she was Italian, one of them knowing the way things worked. Whatever the reason, they became distant, reserved, arms crossed, wanting to hear more about my story and why I was here.

Ombretta stood at center stage. In one hand she held the copy of the family photo and in the other Ferdinando's family tree, which showed my origins rooted in Rotondella. Speaking in rapid-fire Italian, she pivoted in a circle from one group to another as she recounted the major facts, over and over again. Her tiny body was lost among the pack of men, her blond hair bobbing among a mass of dark wool caps. She was clearly in charge, and the men listened attentively to her story of this American woman whose nonna was her North Star, her point of reference. Ombretta explained, "Her nonna, Carmela Perciante, protected her, was her refuge. Her nonna told her stories of Rotondella—working in the fields and carrying barrels of water on her head from the fountain at the foot of the mountain. Lee-bee came to Italy knowing no one. She studied Italian for four weeks before making this trip to find her nonna's home. I came to help her."

The men shifted their gaze toward me, some with admiring looks—*Brava! Good for her, coming all this way from the United States to find family*—while others seemed to say, *What a foolish American. She comes to a small village in the south of a country where she can't even speak the language to find the trace of someone who left more than eighty years ago.*

Although the men seemed interested, they were also careful, reserved. I thought about when Uncle Tony told me, "You ask too many questions. There are some things you don't need to know." Maybe this was the mindset in Rotondella. Maybe no one would answer our questions and, if they remained silent, how would I ever find out anything about Nonna? I also remembered Cornelisen's book, where she described how people of the South held true to *omertà*—a word that means, *I know many things, but I say nothing.*

Without Ombretta, I would have been overwhelmed and fearful. I was the intruder, the foreigner on foreign soil. With Ombretta, under the umbrella of her protection, I felt safe. She knew about *omertà*, about the ways of the South, and about the wariness of the people. She was Italian.

While Ombretta was occupied with the men in the piazza, I moved away from the confusion and stood alone to examine the village. To my left: pharmacy and tobacco shop; straight ahead: town hall and coffee bar; to my right: church and shops. From the central piazza where I stood, several narrow and cobbled streets radiated outward like an intricate spiderweb, each leading to pockets of houses built in a steady succession of high and higher. I felt as if Nonna were standing next to me: "Nonnared, you finally find my home. *Brava! Ma* you know not'-a-ting of life in t'is place. *Stai attenta.*"

With Nonna's voice in my head, I turned my back to the town

and looked out toward the sea. Barren regions, brown and parched, dominated the view. The land was a patchwork quilt with squares of trees, bordered by mounds of dirt, bordered by fields of yellow wheat, bordered by desolate patches of ground. The sea, only five miles away as the crow flies, gleamed blue in the distance, but for Nonna it was a day's journey by foot over the rough, winding terrain. To her, the sea seemed impossible to reach.

I could almost feel Nonna's fingers lifting my chin so that she could look into my eyes and remind me to pay attention. In my mind, I whispered back to her, *I'll be careful, Nonna. Don't worry. Ombretta is with me.*

A cacophony of voices rose behind me and interrupted my imaginings. Turning toward the noise, I counted more than fifteen men surrounding Ombretta, but now the *poliziotto* had arrived. He was dressed handsomely in full police regalia: navy-blue uniform with red and yellow ribbons and gold medals, the blue rim of his white cap edged with a bright yellow cord.

Where did he come from? And why was he talking with Ombretta? Were we in trouble? Maybe we had caused a ruckus, but we had done nothing wrong, certainly nothing illegal. Unless I parked illegally? I rushed to her side, and she shot me a look like, *Would you please stay near me? I'm here for you.*

The *poliziotto* addressed us with respect, but also with an air that combined curiosity with investigative inquiry. Although I understood not one word, I stood next to Ombretta and nodded as if I understood everything. I thought that was the least I could do to support her. No one needed to know I was a total bystander in my own story.

Ombretta held her ground, speaking directly and courteously to the policeman, showing him the picture of my nonni and the hand-drawn family tree. She told him the last names Perciante and LaGuardia, but his face registered no recognition. He simply smiled a half smile and listened attentively.

To our right, the men started shifting their positions to allow space for yet another man to enter. Ombretta looked at me with wide eyes, as if to say, *How many men are coming to meet us?* She whispered to me that maybe her phone calls preceding our visit had put the townspeople on guard, or possibly created interest to see whose family might be related to the American woman. "I don't know if there's a problem or not, Lee-bee," she said in a quiet and serious tone. "But just stay next to me. Don't talk. Even though no one speaks English to us, someone might understand it. We don't want to offend anyone."

The new man, with thinning gray hair, bushy eyebrows, and dark eyes that shifted back and forth as he took in everything, reminded me of the way Uncle Tony played poker. Like him, this man knew how to read faces. He took his place next to the policeman. The onlookers fell silent. They were waiting to hear how these two would respond to us, if they would help us or send us packing.

I took a step closer to Ombretta as if to protect her, but I could see by the glint in her blue eyes that she was already on high alert. I could feel the mood in the piazza changing from mischievous curiosity to a keen desire to know if we were really who we said we were. So much was different here than when I had arrived in Florence, where no one paid any attention to me.

The man introduced himself as Salvatore the Tailor. In my mind, I thought he could be part of the Mafia, or maybe the Black Hand. I don't know why I thought this, but it was true that he had influence over the other men, including the policeman. Maybe my imagination was running away with me, but it was a fact that the men stood apart and gave him space to get close to us. It was a fact that his eyes narrowed, taking in all that was happening. It was a fact that he greeted the men in a sophisticated yet familiar way as he shook hands and made direct eye contact. I had seen this behavior many times in my past: an attitude that speaks of power, connections, and family ties. I saw my own father and Uncle Tony act this way, and my guess was that Nonno Vincenzo had a similar presence. Shoulders back, feet apart, arms crossed, wearing a tie to separate him from the others.

Ombretta never faltered. She explained to the policeman and the tailor why we were there and, as evidence, showed the photo and sketch of my family tree. I stood mute, but a sudden fear flashed through my mind. Dialect! What would happen if someone started speaking dialect and Ombretta couldn't understand? As quickly as the thought had come to me, it faded when I saw a genuine smile radiate from both men. Salvatore the Tailor shook Ombretta's hand and then mine before turning to leave, waving backhand the way Nonna used to, by bending his arm at the elbow and waving with his palm inward, facing his shoulder. He left the same way he had arrived, moving through the center of the group as he wished us a good day and welcome, *Buona giornata e benvenute.*

The men seemed satisfied that we were harmless and, with the blessing of the tailor and the policeman, they began drifting away, some returning to their prior positions in the piazza while others wandered down a nearby street. The policeman told us that the town hall was now closed; however, he would see us tomorrow at the *commune,* where we would search for birth records of Vincenzo and Carmela. He explained that we couldn't leave the car in the piazza and told Ombretta where to park. If we needed anything, we should go to the local coffee bar owned by Giambattista, where he assured us, we would find help. Then he left.

Ombretta and I stood alone in the piazza. In the end, we had been treated like rock stars. The tailor had even told us to visit his shop, where he would be honored to give us a welcoming gift.

"There sure was a lot of fuss about us," I mused while looking around, hands on my hips. "I don't think they get many visitors."

Ombretta nodded in agreement. "I'm sure you're right. It's a very small village and I don't think many Americans come here. As you can see, it's not an easy journey."

"What did we learn about Carmela?" I asked while shifting my seven-zippered bag onto my right shoulder. During all those prior conversations, none of which I understood, I was sure Ombretta must have discovered some possible links.

She looked at me wide-eyed, as if my question made no sense.

"Did you find my family?" I looked right back with my own wide eyes.

Clasping her hands in front of her chin as if in prayer, she shook them up and down at me. Then, with a touch of anger in her voice, she said, "We didn't learn anything yet. We just arrived! What could we know? What could I have found out? It's a small town, yes, but there is a lot of research that must be done."

"But there were many men who said they have the same last names as mine," I shot back. "I can't believe that we came this entire distance and no one has any idea about my family."

Ombretta's tone sharpened. "You must look at things through their eyes. You dropped in on them on a search, out of the blue, from America. I am an Italian woman from the North asking questions about their people. We need to stay here and show them they can trust us. They could be suspicious. We don't understand anything about this place, but we will. You need to have patience."

"What could they think?" I objected. "I'm obviously searching for family. Look at me—I have photos and names. How could anyone doubt me?"

"You're American and you think answers should be quick and efficient," she countered. "This is the South of Italy. You're a stranger. Why should they trust you? The townspeople could be thinking many things. We could be from the government assessing families and businesses for unpaid taxes. They don't know. They might think you are here to claim some inheritance or property from a distant relative. We could be in the wrong town. There are many small villages in the South that experienced emigration. What they do know is that we are not from here and that we are asking about them."

I opened my mouth to protest, but she held up her open palm, like my father, who stopped conversations with a mere flick of his hand.

"Let's visit the tailor," she said, fed up with our conversation. "I can tell. He *has* to know more than he says."

As we turned and began making our way out of the piazza, a tiny old woman with a hawk-shaped nose and dressed from head to toe in black with a babushka wrapped around her head and knotted under her fleshy chin stood directly in front of Ombretta. The woman arched her back aggressively, looked up at Ombretta with narrowed squinty eyes, and huffed something. Ombretta responded quickly, "No, *signora*, no." The woman shook her head angrily and shuffled off.

"What did she ask you?"

"She asked if we were refugees from Albania." Ombretta shook her head in disbelief. "I guess she thought the rips in my Versace jeans were from being old and not from fashion. We are strangers here. Pay attention to what you do." Nonna's words, in my imagined conversation, came back to me: "*Ma* be careful, you know not'-a-ting of life in t'is place. *Stai attenta.*"

Reprimanded, I followed Ombretta silently down the hill to the tailor's shop. When we entered, he smiled pleasantly and took obvious pride in presenting each of us with a lovely scarf: blues for Ombretta and earth tones for me. He had obviously taken note of our coloring when we met him in the piazza.

Maybe he was just kind by nature, or maybe he wanted to keep tabs on us, but for whatever reason he had already planned our evening: We were to cancel any hotel reservations we had previously booked and stay the night in Rotondella in the rooms above Giambattista's coffee bar, where we would be centrally located, near the main piazza and next to the *comune*. The village's restaurant was closed today, but he had already called the owner and told her to open the door and expect us at eight p.m. for dinner. In the meantime, we were to go and check into our rooms. He apologized in advance because he would not be at the town hall in the morning to help with our search for birth and marriage documents, but he assured us the mayor would be. We were not to worry about anything, he told Ombretta reassuringly, because he would take care of us for as long as we were in Rotondella.

Wrapping our new scarves loosely around our necks, we retraced our steps back up the hill to our car and the piazza. As we were passing yet another church, I asked Ombretta if she would move the car while I went inside to pray. With a roll of her eyes and a head nod, she continued to trudge up the mountain to the car. I entered the church, where I lit three votive candles in front of the altar to San Antonio of Padua, the patron saint of Rotondella, whom Nonna called *San Antó:* the first candle for Mom and Dad, the second for my sons Jeff and Jeremy, and the third for Ombretta—for her continued strength and patience with me.

Then, on my knees in front of the statue of the Blessed Mother, I prayed that I would find relatives in Rotondella and become a part of a bigger family. *La famiglia.* The importance of that word to every Italian, but especially here in the South, was embedded in my soul. *La famiglia* was community, well-being, protection, prosperity, identity, and a way of life. When you let someone in as a family member, you hand her the key to your front door and entrance to your heart. It is possibly the most exclusive community in the world. I wanted to be part of *la famiglia,* a place where I could share stories about my nonna and our family and learn whatever I could about my grandparents.

I rose, genuflected, made the sign of the cross, and could almost hear Nonna say, *"Pazienza,* Nonnared. Go slo-slo." I touched her ring, which I'd worn on my right hand ever since she had given it to me, prayed silently for her guidance, and exited.

Chapter 13: Giambattista's Inn

Ombretta, already in front of Giambattista's bar, was puffing on a cigarette and pacing in front of our two roller bags, which she had lugged from the car. She had draped her jean jacket over her shoulders because of the chill in the evening air. As I approached her, I heard sounds of clanking plates and smelled the familiar scent of tomato sauce. The church bells of Sant'Antonio rang in the distance, and I remembered Nonna telling me she was allowed to walk only as far as the sound of the chimes.

We entered the coffee bar through a full-length, multicolored beaded curtain, and the swishing sound announced our presence. Giambattista, a short, rotund man with gray hair framing the crown of his bald head, greeted us with a deep, welcoming *"Buona sera, signore."* I had not seen him in the piazza at our arrival, but it was obvious he knew who we were because he spoke immediately to Ombretta, and I heard the words *Americana, famiglia,* Perciante, and LaGuardia. He offered us an espresso, and we both thanked him kindly but declined. With this expected Italian hospitality out of the way, he and Ombretta began discussing room rental. We wanted two rooms, each with a private bathroom. Did he have them?

With this, he leaned his head back, held his expansive belly with both hands, and laughed heartily. In perfect Italian, he explained to Ombretta, who explained to me, that his "inn" had only two rooms. Both were unoccupied, but there was only one bathroom with only a tub, located in the hallway. There he also stored water, toilet paper, and cleaning supplies. His smile seemed to say, *You're not in the big city anymore, ladies. You're in Rotondella, and these are the only accommodations in town.*

And the price?

With this, a woman suddenly appeared from behind a door in back of the bar. She huddled with him, speaking a language I had never heard: a guttural, harsh sound, not the soft, musical Italian I was used to. I assumed she was his wife. Maybe she was Greek or Arabic or Turkish. When they spoke together, they used her language.

I looked at Ombretta. "What language are they speaking?" I asked naively. "Do you know what they're saying?"

Banging her hands against her legs in exasperation, she whipped her head to the side, walked away from me, and then turned quickly. "Dialect!" she practically yelled. "I can't understand one word."

Dialect! All that Ferdinando, the youth hostel owner in Rome, and my Italian teacher, Paola, had explained was true. We were now face-to-face with the reality of their warnings. This was why Nonna had refused to teach me Italian. Dialect was all she knew. She was trying to protect me from discrimination. Until this moment, everyone we had met—the tailor, the policeman, and the men in the piazza—had spoken classical Italian. Now I was afraid. If Ombretta couldn't understand, what would become of us? How would we know what to do if we didn't understand the language? I stood silent, anxious, watching this scene unfold.

Ombretta began pacing quickly back and forth, alternating between glaring at the couple and looking at me with wide eyes, chin rigid, and lips pursed into one thin line. She was a boiling pot ready to explode and, after another minute of being shut out of the negotiation, she took a bold step toward the couple, raised her voice above theirs, and began speaking to the duo in Italian. But even with her assertive tone, they totally ignored her and continued their conversation about money in dialect.

As quickly as it started, it ended. The woman disappeared through the same door from which she had entered. Calmly and courteously, Giambattista returned his attention to Ombretta, saying politely and, once again in perfect Italian, that one room costs one-hundred-fifty-five-*mila lire* and two rooms cost double, but we were obliged, he explained, to take both rooms because one room had only a single bed and the other a double, "but not big enough for two women."

Agitated, Ombretta recounted the situation to me. "The cost for both rooms is approximately one hundred and seventy dollars, a very high price to pay in a village like Rotondella, and to share a bathroom that is a storage area. But I recommend we pay and stay here. We need help tomorrow in the *comune* to find documentation about your grandparents, and we cannot offend anyone here, especially him. I'm sure he knows everyone."

She stopped and said frankly, "But you are paying the bills as we agreed, so it is your decision."

It was now my turn to stop the conversation by raising my open hand. This gesture breathed time into the air, allowed me to stop the action, decompress, and reflect on all that had happened. Ombretta had made every decision up to this point, and I trusted her knowledge and judgment. I would have been lost without her good sense, language fluency, tenacity, and hard work.

I considered my options: One, we could negotiate a better price. Two, we could call hotels in neighboring villages, compare rates, and then decide where to stay. But my third option was limited to paying the stated price. I realized that, as an American, I was totally out of my realm, especially in this remote village in the South of Italy, where I couldn't even understand the language. Many people thought all Americans were rich. Nonna had told me that men who returned to Rotondella after working four or five years in America had pockets full of money, oftentimes enough to buy the land they once worked. I was sure the cost was too high, but I was also sure Ombretta was correct.

I shrugged my shoulders and nodded my head up and down: I would pay. Giambattista seized upon this universal sign of consent and like a maestro waved his arm to the right, directing us up the stairs to our rooms. We had no trouble finding them because there were only three rooms off the narrow hallway: two bedrooms and one bath. Our rooms were minimal but clean: mine had a single bed, one wooden chair, a hook on the back of the door for my coat and clothes, and a white plastic globe covering the ceiling light, while Ombretta had a double bed, a chair, a freestanding wardrobe, and one stark overhead light bulb. The silver lining was that my room had a small iron balcony with a bird's-eye view of the piazza and the entire undulating vista.

Ombretta was exhausted and ready for dinner. "We've had a long day and will have an even bigger day tomorrow," she said while grabbing her towel and toiletry bag, heading to the communal bathroom. *"Andiamo.* We haven't eaten since breakfast."

Ten minutes later, we were saying goodbye to Giambattista, who informed us there were no keys to our rooms. "Just enjoy your dinner. No worries. I'll be here when you return." I glanced at Ombretta with wide eyes because this would have been unheard of in the States: to stay at a hotel with no key. Ombretta shook her head at me as if to say *keep quiet,* and she led the way out of the bar.

We walked through winding and narrow stone streets, each more steeply sloped as we climbed. In some spaces, when I reached my arms out to the sides, I could stand in the center of the road and touch both opposing walls at the same time. We easily found Via Giotto, climbed the steps into La Mangiatoia's top floor, where we happily discovered a large rustic room with many wooden tables surrounded by six or more chairs. I could imagine families sitting and sharing meals as we did at Nonna's home.

The restaurant was empty, so we seated ourselves at a square table to the left of the entrance and near a window. Within two minutes, a woman in a white chef's jacket and matching bonnet, strands of gray, frizzy hair framing her gentle face, came from the kitchen, and approached us shyly. As promised, she had come to prepare our dinner.

Ombretta, seizing this opportunity to collect information that might help us in our quest, immediately launched into my background, telling the woman that my grandparents were born in Rotondella and we had come to find family members. As proof, she showed the woman the picture, and explained that Carmela was a Perciante and Vincenzo was a LaGuardia. The woman bent close to examine the photo and turned toward me, squinting her eyes and studying my face, as if looking for a resemblance between me and someone she knew, but she said nothing about recognizing the names Perciante or LaGuardia or the possibility that she might know members of my family. *Omertà* ruled. She stood there silent, waiting.

Realizing that there were no answers to be found from this woman, Ombretta spoke to me in a clipped voice, interrupting my studying of the menu, where I found familiar words like *frzzul, mddich, u pastizz,* and *gnummaredd.*

"We need to order, Lee-bee. I know you want to experience all of Rotondella, so I recommend that we try the traditional dishes of this region. How about if I ask the *signora* to bring us whatever she thinks is best?"

"Yes," I said with a smile to both women. "Perfect."

What followed brought Nonna into this dining room. We started with local red wine, strong and robust, made from their harvest of *aglianico* grapes. Ombretta, true to her mission that I should understand as much as possible about the region, explained the history of these southern grapes. "They were not born in Basilicata. The Greeks brought them here. When the Romans took control, they called the grape *Ellenico,* until years later it found its final name as *Aglianico.* It's a strong, bold wine. Different from ours in Tuscany." She raised her glass, and we toasted, *Cincin!*

A basket of thick yellow slices of bread came next, not the typical white unsalted bread of Tuscany. Ombretta explained that it was yellow from the color of the regionally grown wheat. I poured a little local olive oil, opaque, syrupy, and amber-colored, onto my bread, and when I bit into it, my teeth tingled with its dense, full-bodied flavor. Appetizers came next, including several types of home-cured spicy salami, thin slices of *falaoni* filled with potatoes and onions, along with generous portions of eggplant, peppers, and mushrooms, all cured under oil.

Hearty pasta called *frzzul,* just like Nonna used to make, was served next with rich red *sugo.* The main course was *capretto lattante,* milk-fed baby goat, and it melted in my mouth. Oven-roasted potatoes, crisp and deliciously crusty on the outside but still soft inside, were heaped onto a separate platter. I remembered Nonna making potatoes just like this by adding a bit of water to the roasting pan, a technique I never perfected. After this main course, salad arrived in a communal bowl with two small plates for serving.

I smiled with satisfaction because this salad was the Nonna kind, made with dandelion greens, cut celery, a few carrot slices, chopped tomatoes, and mixed with olive oil, a touch of red wine vinegar, and a little salt. She always said salad must be eaten after a meal because it aided in the digestion.

Many of the foods were strange to Northern-born Ombretta, but not to me. Nonna had prepared these foods as part of her daily menu. The thick texture of the pasta on my teeth, the garlic-and-tomato scent of the sauce, and the delicate crust of the *falaoni* all reminded me of Nonna. Food was Nonna's gift of love, her way of keeping her family close. But it was also her connection to her past, to her Italian ancestry. This was how she had lived in Rotondella, and how she continued to live in America. She knew no other way. In a recent survey among Italian Americans to determine what made them feel most "Italian," many said, *our food, our pasta*. This was Nonna's enduring bond with her home.

I lost myself in memories of Nonna, eating heartily from every dish, while Ombretta picked at her food and talked with Ferdinando on her mobile phone. I could imagine that she was recounting each and every detail about our trip, and he must have been interested because they talked a long time. When she ended the call, she explained to me that Ferdinando would call Uncle Patsy to report our status and keep the family informed. Neither of us wanted dessert or espresso, so Ombretta asked the *signora* for the check.

The cost of the two dinners totaled less than fifteen dollars. To thank the woman for her efforts, for opening the restaurant just for us, and for preparing a meal that I so enjoyed, I left a generous tip. On our way out the door, Ombretta nodded goodbye with a quick *buona sera, signora*. I couldn't help but lean over and kiss both of her plump cheeks.

Chapter 14: The Search

The following morning, Ombretta, already dressed and ready for the day, knocked at my door at seven thirty, saying, *"Sbrigati*. It's time for breakfast." I had stayed awake until two o'clock in the morning to write in my journal and document all that had happened. Bathing and dressing quickly, I joined her downstairs by eight fifteen, where we both had a cappuccino and a brioche with Giambattista and Enrico, the policeman from yesterday, now casually dressed in a green cardigan sweater. As usual, Ombretta was at the center of conversation, toggling quickly between English and Italian. Without her, I could understand nothing; with her, Rotondella opened to me.

The two men were full of good cheer and chatter, although they still gave no indication of knowing anything about my family. All the people whom we had met reflected a similar attitude: welcoming but protective; wanting to hear news but not wanting to give news; remaining close but distant at the same time.

When the town hall opened at nine o'clock, Ombretta and I were already waiting at the front door. Francesco Pancrazio, the town hall administrator, unlocked and opened the main door to the *comune,* greeted us kindly, and explained that he had been expecting us; by this time, I wasn't surprised. Dressed in a plaid sport coat, an open-collared blue shirt, and navy slacks, he led us down a dimly lit, butter-colored hallway into his office.

In many cities in Italy, the town hall is difficult to negotiate because it houses a beehive of government services, including immigration, health care, foreign assistance, and registries of births, deaths, and marriages, but Rotondella's *comune* was small and personal.

Once again, Ombretta took the lead, explaining that I had traveled from the States to find family records of Carmela Perciante and Vincenzo LaGuardia. Signor Pancrazio's face, like all the others, registered no recognition of either surname. Ombretta also showed him both the photo and the family tree.

"OK, fine." He rubbed his hands together in anticipation. "Let's begin with your documents to confirm that your grandparents were born here," he said in rapid-fire Italian. Ombretta translated into English, waiting for my response, which she would dutifully translate back.

I wasn't prepared for this request, the first time anyone had ever asked me for legal verification. "I have nothing like a passport or identity card, but I'm sure she was born here. She told me so."

Ombretta translated with a professional tone, but the seeds of doubt had been planted. I had traveled all the way from the United States to Rotondella based solely on the stories that Nonna had recounted. Signor Pancrazio was probably following government protocol in asking for documentation because my grandparents must have had some official papers to leave Italy, board a boat in Naples, and successfully negotiate their way through Ellis Island. Maybe Nonna had given this information to Uncle Tony, who took care of her legal affairs after Vincenzo's death, but I had never thought to ask him.

"I'm positive we'll find her birth certificate here," I said, my voice confident. "She was born on April 5, 1889. Just look, please."

Signor Pancrazio arched his eyebrows as if to say, *We'll see if what your grandmother told you was correct.* Underneath this look, I also read another: *You came all this way because of something an illiterate woman told you, but you have nothing to prove this claim; only an old nonna's memory and your trust that you remembered her stories accurately, including names of places and dates.* Another thought probably also went through his mind: that this could be a wild-goose chase, a waste of his morning.

"Your request isn't so easy as you might think," he explained, rubbing the back of his neck. "The records you need are not entered into a computer, so I have to search the oldest archives, found only in books. In 1889, few people in the South of Italy could read or write. All information had to be handwritten and their pages bound: They are now stored in locked cabinets. I'm a little skeptical about this search with no documentation at all."

Ombretta's strained facial expression told me that she was anxious about his ambivalence, but I knew she would not be easily derailed. In an animated voice, she began detailing how much effort we had put into this trip. "Lee-bee came from America for this one reason. I accompanied her to help her on this very important search for family. Her nonna was her point of reference. I'm sure you understand. This has been her lifelong dream: to find her roots."

"But you never know after all these years." He shook his head, lighting up a cigarette and exhaling a cloud of smoke that fogged his face. "Records get lost and misplaced; it's been more than one hundred years, yes?" He stared at me above the brown rims of his eyeglass frames, as if driving home his point.

Then he added, "Have you searched the church records yet?" Not waiting for an answer, because he probably already knew we hadn't, he continued, "That's where you should start. If you find her Baptism certificate, then come back here. In those years, everyone was baptized. Everyone in Italy was Catholic." With this, I thought about all the public places—restaurants, coffee bars, and even Giambattista's inn—where I had seen displayed blessed Easter Palm and photos of Pope John Paul II, Padre Pio, and Jesus the Sacred Heart.

Standing behind his desk with his left hand in his pant's pocket and his right hand jiggling the cabinet keys, he looked deep in thought, as if he was contemplating his next move in a chess game. Ombretta started to pace and puff on her cigarette and Signor Pancrazio dragged on his, while I stood silent, not knowing what to do or how to help. We were at a critical juncture, and the only one moving her feet was Ombretta.

As if on cue, Enrico entered jauntily, dressed again in full police uniform. Ombretta capitalized on his entrance, greeting him kindly and by name. She thanked him for his assistance as if he were an accomplice in our quest, her tune sounding something like, *Thank you for coming to help us. . . . We've made this difficult journey. . . . You saw the photo and the family tree. . . . Her nonna was Perciante.* Like the second instrument in a two-piece band, Signor Pancrazio chimed in with his counterpoint against this main melody, and I imagined his tune sounding something like, *Year 1889. . . . more than one hundred years ago. . . . They don't have any documents. . . . It could be a waste of a whole day.*

Enrico the Policeman smiled first at Ombretta and then at me. He knew what we were doing and decided to play along. He encouraged the dubious administrator with one word, *"Dai,"* that, loosely translated, means, *Oh, come on.* The tone in the room shifted and lightened; Signor Pancrazio shrugged his shoulders, stubbed out his cigarette, and walked into an adjacent room. The search began.

After fifteen minutes of keys rattling, metal doors banging, and cardboard boxes thudding as they were moved, stacked, and restacked, he reemerged with his arms wrapped around two large brown leather-bound books, each one at least two feet tall, one foot wide, and nine inches thick. The coffee-colored edges of each page curled at the corners with age. He heaped both volumes onto the desk. Although I couldn't see any notations on the front covers, I reasoned they must be arranged in chronological order, so he must be starting with January 1889 or earlier. Before he had time to open the cover of the first book, Ombretta was already at his side, joining him in the search to scan each delicate page for the name Carmela Perciante. The policeman placed himself in front of the desk, leaning over the book, reading the pages upside down. Three Italians hovered over the huge record books, looking for one woman's name.

I stood back, watching every hand and eye movement as Ombretta, Enrico the Policeman, and Signor Pancrazio scanned each leaf of paper, all the while praying that Nonna had remembered the correct date of her birth, and also that I had recorded it correctly.

One brittle page after another: I listened to the crackling, the tick of a clock, the exhaling of cigarette smoke, a dog barking in the distance, and the occasional slam of a car door somewhere outside. I didn't want to interrupt. I was the American who couldn't read the words on the pages but whose history was there. I remembered high school religion classes, when nuns taught us that cloistered monks dedicated their lives to the transcription of the Bible and sacred music for posterity's sake. In this case, I was posterity and could be the grateful recipient. I also thought about people who searched for their roots only to discover that their written history in some book had been destroyed because of war, fire, or flood. I prayed that Carmela's folio had outlasted the ravages of time.

Signor Pancrazio was growing frustrated, puffing more vigorously on a newly lit cigarette. I was afraid he was thinking that this was an endless task and that Carmela had either been born in another year or in some other Southern Italian village.

As if a stage manager was directing this scene and true to the tailor's word, the mayor arrived, a slender, handsome man dressed smartly in a gray suit and tan leather belt with matching shoes. Ombretta quickly greeted him and thanked him for coming, praising Signor Pancrazio and the policeman for their help in our search. The mayor smiled with pleasure, surveyed what was happening, and took his place behind Signor Pancrazio, looking over his shoulder and bringing a renewed level of enthusiasm to our group.

Another page turned and now there were four people—the administrator of the *comune*, Ombretta, the policeman, and the mayor—searching for one woman's name. They were trying, and that's all I could ask for.

The first book was heaved aside, the second tome opened. Ombretta looked at me, shook her head back and forth in a worried way, jabbed out her cigarette in the ashtray, and continued scanning.

Nonna, where are you? I prayed silently, *You never let me down; you were always waiting for me. Where are you today?* I was feeling desperate, knowing that both time and patience were growing slim.

My prayer was interrupted when Signor Pancrazio exclaimed, triumphantly raising both hands in the air, *"Eccoci!"* Here we are! I rushed to his desk and stood behind Ombretta, towering over her head and seeing a mass of illegible words. But there were two words I could read: *Carmela Perciante*. Nonna was here! Her name was on this page. She was born in Rotondella. Here was proof.

While I stared silently at her name, registry number 84, Ombretta translated aloud:

> *In the year 1889, today 5 April at the time 10:20 am in the City Hall in front of me Giuseppe LaBattaglia, on behalf of the mayor . . . appeared Vincenzo Perciante (son of Giovanni), a worker in the field, resident of Rotondella, who declared to me that at 8:30 am on the first day of April . . . was born a baby of female sex that he is presenting to me and to whom he gave the name Carmela.*

With tears in my eyes, I reverently touched the page, as if touching it made Carmela alive again. I looked at Ombretta, whose blue eyes were brimming with tears, and hugged her, nearly lifting her off her feet, whispering, "Thank you, thank you."

Our goal reached, the mayor patted Signor Pancrazio's back with obvious pride, bid us goodbye with an efficient, *"Buon proseguimento,"* wishing us good luck with our future plans. He instructed Signor Pancrazio to make a copy of the document for me as a keepsake, satisfied that his *comune* had preserved the files in good condition and that my trip to Rotondella produced the results I had hoped for. Enrico the Policeman smiled genuinely, shook our hands with a sincere, "Arrivederci, signore," waved backhand, and followed the mayor out the door.

We were alone—Signor Pancrazio, Ombretta, and me—all content with having found Carmela, one hundred and ten years after her birth. The *comune*'s records had not failed. But I was confused about Nonna's birthdate. "Why," I asked Ombretta, who translated for Signor Pancrazio, "did Nonna tell me her birthday was April 5 when she was really born, according to the certificate, on April 1?"

"Ah, that's easy," replied Signor Pancrazio speaking to Ombretta, who continued her simultaneous translation. "During those years, children were born at home with a midwife. The father and other children worked in the fields. There was no choice. They could not take time away from their work for the birth of another child or official registration."

He turned to his computer and pulled up the calendar for 1889, pointing to the screen. "Ah, just as I thought. Your grandmother was born on the first day of April, a Monday. No *contadino* could stay home on Monday. Your great-grandfather, your *bisnonno*, registered Carmela's birth on Friday, the last day of the week, so April 5 became her official birth date, which was the day of registry."

Ombretta continued, explaining that the document was read to my great-grandfather and witnessed by two men. She pointed to the bottom of the birth certificate and translated: *We read the present certificate to all because they couldn't sign because they were not able to sign.*

"And you know why," Signor Pancrazio jumped back into the conversation, glancing over the top of his glasses as Nonna used to, "all three men—your *bisnonno* and the two witnesses—couldn't sign their names and why everything had to be read to them?" Waiting only long enough for Ombretta to translate, he continued, "They never learned how to read, write, or even sign their names. No one went to school in those days, or I should say extremely few, and only the wealthy. In 1859, the Casati Act was passed, making education mandatory through the third grade. At that time, illiteracy in the South was more than eighty percent, and it took over fifty years to reduce this number by half. The people in Rotondella had to work. There was no time for school."

My memories were falling into place. I remembered Nonna tugging my ponytail when I was seven, lecturing me that I had to study hard and telling me how proud she was of her daughter, "Your mamma is always one of t'e best in school. *Oye,* she is smart." It wasn't until today that I realized the full import of Nonna's stories, and why she signed her name with an X. My nonni never had the chance to go to school because they were *contadini*. Even as children, they had to work, and the primary work in Rotondella was in the fields.

Ombretta's voice brought me back to the present. Her desire for me to understand was paramount. "Lee-bee, the fields were both Carmela's life's sentence and her family responsibility. All *contadini* during that time worked in the fields from early morning until late in the evening—from before the sun came up and until after the sun went down. It was their life. This was true not only for your grandparents but for many of the people who lived at that time. She was tied to the ground like a mule tied to an iron bar, but at the same time this was her world. It was all she knew."

Signor Pancrazio nodded in agreement. He cradled the ledgers in both arms and began walking out of the room to return them safely to storage.

"Lee-bee," Ombretta raised her voice in a leading way, "is there anything else you want to find out?" She lifted her chin toward Signor Pancrazio's exit. "How about your grandfather's records?" she said, attempting to refocus me before we lost his help.

"Oh, of course." I followed Ombretta's lead. "Signor Pancrazio, could we please try to find my nonno's birth document? I'd hate to have come all this way without finding him, too," I admitted, as if finding the certificate would mean that I found his person. "But I'm sorry; I have no idea when he was born. I never asked Nonna."

"*Certo!* That won't be difficult now that we found Carmela." He laughed easily. I breathed a huge sigh of relief although I had no idea why this would be easy.

He returned the books to his desk, found once again Nonna's birth certificate, and pointed to the side panel where, written in very small handwriting under her name, was her marriage information: September 23, 1911, to Vincenzo Gaetano LaGuardia, who was born on February 12, 1886, to mother Laura Fortunato and father Gaetano LaGuardia, *contadino*.

Leaving Nonna's book on his desk, he left the room again and we heard more cabinets clanging. This time, he returned with only one book, the aged pages darkened to the color of caramel. After another careful search and slow turning of pages, Signor Pancrazio and Ombretta found Number 63: Vincenzo Gaetano. My trusty translator read:

> *In the year 1886, today the 12 of February at 3:05 pm in the City Hall in front of me Giuseppe LaBattaglia, on behalf of the mayor . . . appeared Antonia Gialdini of 70 years, midwife, resident of Rotondella, who declared to me that at 9:30 am on 11 February . . . was born a baby of*

male sex that she showed to me and to whom was given the name Vincenzo Gaetano.

As with Nonna's certificate, neither the midwife nor the two male witnesses could read or sign their names. After checking the calendar and finding that February 11 was a Thursday, Signor Pancrazio conjectured that my great-grandfather wouldn't leave the fields to register his son, so the midwife took the responsibility one day after the birth. Work was as essential as breathing. Things were making sense.

In quick order, we found their marriage certificate: Carmela was twenty-two and Vincenzo was twenty-five years old and, as we had anticipated, neither one could sign his name. They both signed with an *X*.

Signor Pancrazio graciously accompanied us to the front door of the *commune*, and he reassured us that he would make copies of the relevant pages. "I have some ideas about people who might be your relatives," he offered tentatively. "Give me time to make some calls. Come back here around four o'clock, and I'll let you know what I find out. I promise nothing, but I'll do my best."

I was sure he knew more than he was willing to tell, but because of *omertà*, as well as his professional position as director of the *comune*, he was cautious. "Signor Pancrazio," I interrupted him as he turned to leave. Speaking English while Ombretta continued translating, I explained, "I'm grateful for your time and effort, but I have another question." He turned, crossed his arms, raised his eyebrows, and waited.

"My grandfather Vincenzo was a field worker, and his father was a field worker. He never went to school and couldn't read, write, or even sign his name. Yet when he arrived in America, he got a supervisor's job in the water company, and within several years of living and working in the States, he paid for my nonna's and her mother's passage from Italy to America, built a three-story brick house on a corner lot, and bought a Model-T Touring car, one of the first in his town. How was that possible?"

Silence. He said nothing, but I saw a spark in his eyes that said something. He looked at Ombretta with a conspiratorial eye raise, accompanied by a quick shoulder shrug. She averted her eyes, searching the ceiling as if she were suddenly interested in architecture, while never missing a beat in translation. They obviously knew something.

I was not about to be left out, so I tried again. "Why do you have such a look on your face?"

"*Boh.*" His voice held a smile. "What look? I have no look. I know nothing." Then he said more seriously, "But you must think about something: Your grandfather had no education, and when he arrived in America, he probably had little money and could not speak English, yes?"

I nodded in agreement.

"Yet," he continued, "he had a big car, a big job, a big house, and he paid to bring your grandmother and your grandmother's mother from Rotondella." He stopped, as if allowing this information to sink into my head. Like an attorney, he was building a case.

"I don't know what happened to him in America, but I could guess that something must have happened between the time he left Rotondella and Carmela's arrival. In those days, it was normal for the men to go first to America to build a life and a fortune, then to send for their wives and families. My guess is this was true for your family too?"

"Yes," I answered quickly. "According to Ellis Island records, Nonna arrived in the United States three years after Nonno. She was listed on the manifest of the *Duca degli Abruzzi,* which departed from the Port of Naples, age twenty-six, and the ship arrived in New York on November 18, 1915."

"*Brava!* Good that you know that." He nodded professorially. "But for me, I know nothing else. What could I know?"

Turning to Ombretta, he made a sign that I recognized from my youth, one that I hadn't seen in years: He placed his index finger underneath his right eye and pulled the skin down a bit, drawing the eye gently open and downward toward his cheekbone, while he raised both eyebrows upward and turned down the corners of his mouth.

I knew this gesture to mean, *Pay attention: Something is happening.*

But what? I felt lost.

Without waiting a second more, he waved a backhand goodbye and turned on his heels, as I watched the back of his sport coat disappear around the corner.

Chapter 15: Carmela Perciante?

"Tell me," I demanded. "Tell me what Signor Pancrazio thinks. I know you know."

"Lee-bee," Ombretta sighed wearily. "He doesn't know anything. Neither do I. It was a long time ago."

I knew my forceful tone would get me nowhere, so I tried again more softly. "You're right. I understand you're not certain of anything. But tell me, please, what you think."

"OK," she relented. "But let's sit on the bench in the piazza. We both need a little break. It's already been a long morning. I can smoke while we talk."

Once we were settled and she was ready, her lecture began. "You must think about those years at the turn of the century. They were desperate times for the immigrants who left a country they knew to go to a country they didn't. When your grandfather arrived in America, he was uneducated and unskilled. He wasn't able to speak English and knew only his own dialect. Thousands of Italian immigrants were the same. They had no choice but to take filthy jobs, jobs no one else wanted or had refused, even dangerous jobs in dangerous conditions for little money. They lived in hovels in New York City's Little Italy and lots of other places in the States. Pittsburgh might have been like that too. I don't know. What I do know is that Italians often settled together in the same towns to share common foods, religion, and language, but also for help and protection. They had to apply for permits for jobs, driving licenses, documents to stay in America, permission to open businesses, and even access to water and trash removal. These weren't guaranteed to them because they showed up in your country. They had to fill out forms and follow the rules of the system they had entered. Getting out of Naples and through Ellis Island was only the beginning."

She paused to puff on her cigarette. I waited.

"And Carmela, she left Rotondella in November of 1915, when Italy was already fighting in World War I. This was a dangerous time to leave on a ship from Naples. People did what they needed to do to survive."

Finally I heard what she *wasn't* saying. "So, you think that when my grandfather arrived in America he was absolutely desperate and, in order to survive and earn enough money to bring Carmela across the ocean, he became part of the Mafia or the Black Hand? Is that what Signor Pancrazio thinks too?"

"I don't know what he thinks, and I certainly don't know what is true. But even today, our Mafia uses many threats if people don't pay, like the trick of turning off water to homes. In Italy, we don't have this Black Hand—I've never heard of *La Mano Nera* before this—but we certainly have the Mafia." Then she paused, turned toward me, and said in a serious tone, *"Basta.* Enough. I don't want to talk about such things here in the South of Italy. Enough about this until we get back to Florence." Another pause, another drag on her cigarette as she looked out toward the horizon, and then she said under her breath, "But it's a possibility."

I followed her gaze over the barren landscape and the fields where my grandparents had labored. They needed courage to leave their home. Vincenzo had dreamed of starting a new life in America, where he could build a future for Nonna, their children and grandchildren. He arrived in Pittsburgh at the age of twenty-six, illiterate in both Italian and English, with little or no money, and with no job. He had to have felt lost and afraid. When I was a child, Nonna had told me he was a good man, and of course I had believed her. I'm sure she thought he was. In my child's mind, I had imagined him to be a man of justice and integrity, a kind of Robin Hood, the good guy who robbed *from* the Black Hand and *gave* money to the needy. But I wasn't a child any longer. I was an adult who was searching for truth, and the truth was staring me in the face.

*

A deep male voice jarred me out of my thoughts of the Black Hand, the Mafia, and Vincenzo. A handsome young man, whom I recognized from the piazza yesterday, was talking to Ombretta. He was dressed fashionably in a canary yellow windbreaker, jeans, and Nike sneakers, with Ray-Ban aviator sunglasses perched on top of his wavy coal-black hair.

With the pride of accomplishment in her voice, I could tell that Ombretta was explaining that we had already found birth and marriage documents for Carmela and Vincenzo, and that Signor Pancrazio had offered to make some calls to see if I had any relatives who were still living in Rotondella.

"That's why I came to find you," he offered politely, his brown eyes gentle. "I am Gaetano Perciante, though even with the same last name as your friend's grandmother, I don't believe I am related to her family. But if your friend has relatives here, my father will know. He's ninety-one years old and very lucid. I talked with him last night, and he might be able to help your friend. He's in the coffee bar, a short walk from here. I told him that you have a photo and a drawing of her family history. He's willing to look at these and, if he is satisfied with what he sees, he might have something to tell you."

Ombretta quickly translated this information for me. Newly motivated, she was on the trail again and jumped into action. She grabbed her Louis Vuitton backpack and motioned to me with a swift hand movement to pick up my seven-zippered sack and follow her. While Ombretta and Gaetano led the way, deep in a conversation that I couldn't understand, I lagged two steps behind and reflected on all that had happened so far.

This trip to Rotondella was unfolding in ways I hadn't expected. There were so many actors involved in the drama: Signor Pancrazio was making calls, the tailor was omnipresent, Giambattista had our belongings at his inn, the mayor and the policeman were aware of our every movement, my grandfather Vincenzo had probably been associated with the Mafia or the Black Hand, and Gaetano's father was waiting for us. Even if I had wanted to stop the action, things had gone too far already.

Men appeared out of nowhere, as if a circus had come to town. Soon our group of three became a caravan of eleven, moving through the narrow streets leading to the bar. Women, now curious, leaned out of windows above us and yelled, *"Chi é?"*

A man I had never seen before but who was walking next to me, responded in a loud voice, *"Americane."*

Ombretta threw back her head and shouted upward, *"Io sono Italiana. Lei é Americana."*

I looked up and saw five women's faces staring down at me, their dark eyes squinting in suspicious glares. Again, I felt like an intruder. In this sea of Italians, women above me and men around me, I *was* the intruder, the foreigner. I was not one of them.

Gaetano's father, the old man who might know something about my family, must have heard all the commotion because he was already walking slowly out of the bar, accompanied by five more men. Diminutive and unassuming, he was Ombretta's height, dressed neatly in a sport coat and an open-collared shirt, with a full head of snow-white hair and a delicately trimmed mustache. Ombretta, my loyal guide and translator, launched into her explanation, all the while pointing to Ferdinando's family tree and the photo as supporting evidence. She was speaking so fast it sounded like a train whizzing by. I watched her as she waved her arms toward me and emphasized the words Perciante and LaGuardia. The wizened elder listened to every word while studying me out of the corner of his eye. He missed nothing. He was weighing all that he was hearing and seeing. Like Uncle Tony and the tailor, he was reading faces.

He was most interested in the photo and asked Ombretta, *"Posso?"* She handed it to him, and after he focused on each face, he looked at me, I thought, searching for a family resemblance. I considered the possibility that he might have seen the picture before, but I knew that was highly improbable.

While the old man was deciding what to do or say, silence enveloped the street. Even the women above had stopped their chatter. Handing the photo back to Ombretta, he was quiet for what felt like a long time. Everyone was silent, waiting for his verdict. All eyes were on him. Finally, he turned his body toward Ombretta, but he kept his eyes directly on me.

He said something in Italian that I didn't understand; however, I did understand two words: Carmela Perciante. He had said Nonna's name. Why? And the crowd seemed to gasp. Had *omertà* been broken?

When I heard the name Carmela Perciante, spoken out loud on these streets while surrounded by all these gawking people, I couldn't keep anything clear. Was the old man trying to say that Nonna had never left Rotondella? That made no sense. Without waiting for Ombretta to translate, I protested instinctively and immediately. My eyes riveted into his: "Carmela *è morta.*" These words I knew in Italian.

The old man, bewildered by my response, turned to Ombretta looking for some direction. I felt bewildered too. Maybe he hadn't understood my Italian, so once again, without waiting for Ombretta's help or explanation, I repeated the words, the ones I knew to be true, "Carmela *è morta.*"

Ombretta came to my aid, scolding, "Yes, Lee-bee. *Calma!* Sure, you are right. We all know that your Carmela is dead. But this man says there is a woman who lives in this town who has the exact same name as your nonna. Her name is Carmela Perciante. Maybe she's a relative of your family?"

Ombretta paused for a quick moment to give me time to process this new information; then she added, "Her home is nearby. This old man thinks we should walk there now and talk with her. I think we should try. We've come so far. Do you agree?"

Everything was happening so quickly. Was I supposed to believe that I had crossed an entire ocean and traveled to the far edge of a country to find the one woman who bore the exact same name as Nonna?

Along with this thought, two others flashed into my mind in quick succession. First, this town was so small, and news traveled so fast that people knew where we were even before we got there. Ombretta and I had talked with the mayor, the policeman, the tailor, the innkeeper, and the director of the *commune*—even the owner of the restaurant—and not one of them had admitted they knew a woman with the exact same name as the woman for whom I searched. A woman who had been born here and stayed here all her life. Of course they had to have recognized the name Carmela Perciante! Yet no one except Gaetano's father had said anything about her existence. After my twenty-four hours in this village, I was beginning to realize what I had considered to be impossible could be possible.

The second thought was what I knew about Italian customs in naming children: firstborn son after the father's father, firstborn daughter after the father's mother, and secondborn son after the mother's father. But I also remembered that Italians named their children after a fallen hero. For example, my brother Fred, whom we now called JF: James Frederick—James after Nonno Jim and Frederick after my father's beloved brother, who had died in World War II. *A hero,* I thought. *Did Giuseppe, Nonna's brother and my great-uncle, love his sister, my nonna, so much that he named his daughter after her?* This I knew was possible.

A third distant thought was that Gaetano had said his father was ninety-one, so he was born in 1908. Nonna had left in 1915. Her mother, Laura, left eight years later in 1923, when he would have been a teenager. Could it be possible that he remembered them, or one of them? Was that why he seemed so interested in the photo? Could it be possible that he was still withholding information, and that he knew more than he was admitting? Did *omertá* continue to rule?

Biting my bottom lip and shifting my sack onto my left shoulder, I glanced up at the gaggle of women looking down at me and over at Ombretta and the mass of men, especially the old man. I had to say or to do something.

With a shallow nod of my head, I looked at the ground and submitted to Ombretta's good judgment. I was not in a position to deny what was obviously true: There was a woman named Carmela Perciante and she lived here.

Ombretta, Gaetano, and the old man led our cavalcade toward the home of this newly identified Carmela Perciante. The procession of men moved down the stone street with a will of its own. Women's shrill voices clamored above, while men's deep voices surrounded me. I tagged behind Ombretta, walking alone. I needed some space from all the chaos. Everyone seemed to be speaking at the same time, but I could understand nothing of the language. I rolled Nonna's wedding ring round and round on my finger, willing myself to feel her presence.

Our human train stopped in front of a small, one-story house in muted shades of parchment and dusty gray, topped with the obligatory red-tiled roof. To the left of the wooden door was a large open window. The inside was dark.

"The house of Carmela," Gaetano told me in his best English and with a gentlemanly smile, as if to say, *I know everything is moving quickly for you. I know this is hard for you, but it will be OK.* My eyes registered his compassion and I nodded as if in agreement, but then turned quickly, riveting my focus on the window and the black interior.

As I stood in front of the house of a woman named Carmela Perciante, I remembered how Nonna sat in front of the window in her dining room, watched the cars go by, and prayed her rosary. I thought about how we sat on the porch swing the day I ran away, and how she told me not to worry because she would take care of me. For years, I had anticipated finding Rotondella, but I was learning that I could never have adequately prepared for what was happening.

I wished Ombretta were next to me, and as if she had read my mind, I saw her blond hair in my peripheral vision making her way through the crowd to my side. Gaetano took the first step and led the way toward the front door, with me on his heels and Ombretta on mine. The men on the street watched us as if we were characters on a stage. Gaetano knocked gently on the door while Ombretta and I stood behind him. An attractive, middle-aged woman answered. The folds around her eyes and the creases on her forehead showed a look of caution. She must have been wary with the crowd of men gathered in front of the house and three strangers at the door, but then I wondered if someone had already called ahead to forewarn her. Maybe this woman had been expecting us? This, I realized, was more likely.

Gaetano asked permission to enter and the woman nodded,

leading the way down an unlit narrow hallway, her rubber shoes squeaking on the terra-cotta floor. I walked closely behind Gaetano, with Ombretta directly behind me. My thoughts ricocheted like a pinball machine, flicking between excitement that I might find family and fear that this was a wild-goose chase. In addition, I questioned my own behavior: I was entering the house of a woman I didn't know only because she happened to have the same name as my nonna.

I finally realized why no one—not Enrico the Policeman, not the tailor, not Signor Pancrazio, not the mayor, not Giambattista, and not even the owner of the restaurant—had told me about this Carmela Perciante. They were protecting her—an aged woman who had lived her entire life in this village, a woman who lived alone, and a nonna who wasn't accustomed to American visitors barging in—from exactly what was happening to her.

Both Gaetano and Ombretta started talking at the same time. Their voices filled the hallway as they explained simultaneously who we were and why we were here. By this time, Gaetano had heard the story so frequently that he and Ombretta were like two strings on the same violin, playing in harmony. Although I understood nothing of the language, I understood everything of the melody.

We rounded the corner at the end of the hallway and stood in a large kitchen, but the room was in shadows cast by a fire in the fireplace. It was early May, and the flames offered cozy warmth against the chill in the air. As my eyes adjusted to the dim light, I scanned the center of the room but saw no one. If Nonna were here, I knew she would have been seated in the corner between the open window and the fireplace, so that she could study the entire scene as it unfolded outside, but could also stay warm near the flames. I turned toward the far corner of the room.

There she sat. Her coal-black eyes widened with interest. There, I saw no fear. She was examining me as I was examining her. I saw the same nonna housedress, the same hose, the same grandmother shoes, the same black cardigan sweater wrapped around her shoulders, and the requisite grandmother apron hanging nearby. The eyes, the mouth, the nose: I could see my nonna. And her hands nested in her lap, palms up.

Ombretta's voice rose from somewhere close behind me as she spoke directly to the old woman. Ombretta explained in rapid Italian why my Nonna Carmela and Rotondella were important to me, and why I had made this long journey from America. This Carmela listened to every word, and the sweep of her eyes missed nothing. This Carmela was razor-sharp. This Carmela was guarded, judiciously considering every word and every facial expression.

Ombretta handed me the photo of my family, indicating with a quick nod of her head that I was to give it to Carmela. I hesitated. Suddenly, this whole adventure seemed bizarre. I was in a strange woman's kitchen, without even knowing how to communicate with her, invading her space and giving her a picture of my family. I felt embarrassed, ashamed of the intrusion, doubting my tenacious search. Ombretta must have felt my ambivalence because she encouraged me with another nod of her head toward Carmela, this time accompanied by a gentle smile. I approached this new Carmela with two slow steps and tentatively handed her the photo. She looked at me as she reached out her hand, wrinkled with age and with blue veins showing through thin skin.

An immediate and quick twitch happened around her lips, faint but there. If I had not been staring at her, I would have missed it. I felt a flicker of hope.

With a quicker movement than I could have imagined, she was up and standing next to me. She stood as tall as my shoulder, but I knew her size was no indication of her strength of will.

Her hands trembled as she held the photo. I didn't know if the trembling was caused by age, emotion, or some illness. I didn't know if I should reach out to help her or if I should run out of the door.

"This is Grandmother Laura, this is Aunt Carmela, and this is Uncle Vincenzo," she announced clearly in Italian as she pointed to each image on the photo.

Silence. No one spoke. Her words hung in the air.

"No," I whispered, shocked that she recognized the people in the photo and could call them by name. "*Non é possibile.*"

As if battling a troop of Marines, she pulled herself taller to reach her full four feet eleven inches and stared into my eyes. Commanding her space with total authority, she declared in a determined voice, as determined as I knew my nonna to be, *"Questa é la mia nonna Laura, questa é la mia zia Carmela, e questo é il mio zio Vincenzo."*

Her dark eyes looked both at me and through me, as if seeing into my soul and knowing my past. I studied her face more closely: thin, angular, and elegant. This was a woman who knew suffering and who had survived. This was a woman who was independent and refused to leave her home. This was a woman who swept snow wearing only a sweater. This was a woman who had raised her children without a father. This was the matriarch of the family. She really was Carmela Perciante.

Carmela reached out, took my hand, and held it as tears streamed down my face, lost in the blue of my sweater. Then she made *the* gesture, the one that brought Nonna into this room as clearly as if she were standing next to me. This Carmela raised her hand and slid tender fingers down my cheek and whispered gently, *"Non essere triste, mia cara."*

Why did she stroke my face with her fingers? How did she know where to touch? I heard Nonna's voice in my head: "No cry, and no be sad. Why you cry, Nonnared? What goes on?"

Ombretta and Gaetano started talking at the same time, each trying to connect the names of the people in the picture to the history of my newly found Italian family. Their eyes shone with emotion, deep joy, and excitement.

Carmela returned to her chair, and I sat on the floor next to her, just as I had sat next to Nonna when I was a young girl. Reaching up, I held this Carmela's hand while she caressed mine. Ombretta continued her expert translation for me, as Carmela explained her side of the story. "I have the same photograph that you brought here today. That is why my hands shook when I held it. Many years ago, my father, Giuseppe, received the same photograph, and one more. These pictures were all my father had to remember his beloved mother and sister. In fact, both are framed and are on the dresser in my bedroom."

She motioned to the young woman, her *badante*, who went into the bedroom and retrieved two photos, both in silver frames: one was a copy of the picture I had brought and the second was of my family in their Model-T Touring car. I knew this second photo well and remembered it hanging in Nonna's home. My nonna Carmela must have been proud to mail photos home that told of Vincenzo's accomplishments in a single image. Her family had obviously been proud to receive them and had kept them all these years.

"We never heard anything after the photos," Carmela lamented. "We never heard again from Nonna Laura or Zia Carmela. We knew nothing. Tell me. What has happened?"

"I'm sorry, *signora,*" Ombretta responded gently, with sadness in her voice, "but they are all dead. Your Grandmother Laura, your Zia Carmela, and your Zio Vincenzo have all died and are buried in Pittsburgh. Lee-bee's mother is named Laura after your grandmother, and she has two brothers. You have family in Pittsburgh."

"My Zia Porzia and her family?" Carmela asked.

By this time, Ombretta knew well our family tree, and she recognized Porzia as my nonna's beloved older sister. "Porzia is dead, too, but her children are many and living happily in Pittsburgh and Florida."

Certainly Carmela must have known that her grandmother, uncle, and aunts were dead because of the many years gone by, but the words struck her sharply. Sighing and rubbing her knee, she bowed her head in contemplation, as if saying a silent prayer. I studied her hands, gnarled by hard work like Nonna's. She gazed absently into the fire and seemed lost in years of long ago.

The visit was over. I recognized the signs as easily as I remembered Nonna's aching knees, quiet speech, and tired sighs. Ombretta nodded to me. "*Andiamo,* Lee-bee. Carmela has much to think about."

I stood, leaned over, and kissed Carmela on both cheeks. She promised to call her children—the three who lived nearby—to tell them about this reunion so I could meet my cousins. Standing up, a bit more slowly this time, she walked us to her door. She lifted her hand to my forehead and made the sign of the cross three times. This was her holy protection. Her hand slipped onto my cheek, and she stroked my face.

We left Carmela with the knowledge of her family in America. We left her with the knowledge that a great-granddaughter of her grandmother, a searcher of family and truth, had returned to Rotondella. We left her with the knowledge that she and her family had not been forgotten.

Chapter 16: No Mafia in Basilicata

Ombretta, Gaetano, and I walked down the now familiar narrow streets to return to Giambattista's inn. The parade of men had dispersed, and the women had lost interest. When we arrived, it came as no surprise that Giambattista already knew that our morning search at the *comune* had produced birth and marriage documents, and that we had also found the person Carmela Perciante. He and Ombretta talked in a casual way, as if they had been friends for years, while I paid the bill. We bid a fond farewell to our host, explaining that Ombretta's travel agent had made reservations for us at a hotel in Policoro, a nearby seaside village at the base of the mountain, where we would be closer to my cousins' homes and the freeway to return to Foggia airport.

Ombretta and I had three hours of downtime before our afternoon meeting at the town hall with Signor Pancrazio. Gaetano graciously offered to give us a tour of the surrounding area, and we accepted gratefully. He loaded our luggage into the trunk of our car, climbed in the back seat, and explained that he would pick up his own car when we returned to Rotondella. As we descended the steep mountaintop, round and round, we passed goats foraging near the roadside. I wondered, *How was it possible that my great-grandmother Laura walked up these hills with a barrel of water balanced on her head, while knitting at the same time?* Nonna had told me this hard-to-believe fact with great pride in her voice. I had seen pictures of robust women of Rotondella walking up slanted passageways, necks firmly in place, shoulders arched back, as they moved gracefully, all the while balancing on their head a wooden plank with five loaves of bread or a barrel of water.

Our tour began at the sea. Gaetano pointed to the side of a

sandy road. "You can park here. Don't worry. Your car will be safe. Just last week, the police arrested ninety-two people associated with the Mafia. Before this sweep, your tires probably would have been stolen."

Ombretta, translating into English, shot me a look. By this time, I knew to keep my mouth clamped shut.

Gaetano must have seen Ombretta's blue eyes widen and her quick headshake because he added quickly, "But there is no problem. Everyone will be cleared and released soon. Mafia is only in Naples and Sicily. There is no Mafia in Basilicata."

Baffled by his quick turn around, I filed this information into a mental folder labeled JIM THE WATERMAN AND THE MAFIA. This topic was like dancing with shadows.

We walked to the seaside, where Gaetano, a proud maestro, with a broad sweep of his arm presented to us the distant and vast reaches of the Ionian. This was his land and his birthright. The seashore was wide and expansive, dressed in powdery white sand much like the beaches I'd visited in the Caribbean. The Ionian Sea stretched beyond my sight, and I could imagine ancient Greek ships in the distance, sails billowing, carrying Odysseus to Ithaca. I could imagine pirate ships landing on shore to terrorize villagers. I could also imagine how Nonna longed to be exactly where I was standing, to dip her feet into the coolness of the water, and to breathe deeply the salty air. Her words echoed in my head: "T'e sea. I can only look, Nonnared. It is too far for me to reach."

I particularly wanted to see the fields where Nonna had labored. Gaetano explained that he wasn't sure of the exact area, but he would be happy to take us to the major agricultural center. We climbed into the car and drove to a spot where the road opened into an immense expanse of ground that looked like limitless acres, radiating in all directions. In early May, the trees were beginning to bud in various shades of spring green, and vegetable shoots were breaking through the soil. Gaetano told Ombretta, who translated for me, that although wheat and olives were still staple products of the region, modern farming equipment and especially irrigation allowed farmers to grow peach, apricot, apple, and pear trees. Even strawberries.

Vegetables like peppers, eggplant, potatoes, tomatoes, and artichokes were also abundant. "But when your grandparents lived and worked here, life was very different. Without irrigation, fruit trees and many vegetables couldn't be cultivated. Wheat was the major harvest in those days. The work was backbreaking.

"In those years, at the turn of the century," he continued, his voice filled with compassion for the lives of the people who had gone before him, "*contadini* worked fields owned by rich nobles, a few of whom lived in Rotondella, although most lived in Matera or Rome. Bosses, called *padrone,* supervised the work, and the largest portion of the land's produce was paid to the land barons. The *contadini* worked the land with tools—scythes, axes, hoes, picks, mattocks, and shovels—whatever they had. The wealthier of the poor had mules to help carry firewood, equipment, and food, but very few people rode the mule because its strength was also needed to pull the plow. When there was no mule or horse, the father, son, or even mother strapped their bodies into the harness to do the beast's work."

He watched Ombretta with sad eyes as she continued to translate. She nodded her head in agreement as she surveyed the vast terrain. These were not new stories to her.

"Women and girls wore a scarf called a *fular* to protect their heads and faces against the burning sun or chilling winds. Men and boys stuffed their heads into a *cappello,* a woolen or cloth cap, or wore wide-brimmed felt hats to protect them from the scorching sun. In winter, clothes were made of wool; in summer, they were made of flax. Shoes were pieces of leather or wood tied to feet with rope and, in winter and rainy seasons, nails were driven through the base to help grip when walking in the snow, ice, or mud. Mothers knitted woolen stockings to protect their families' legs from the weeds and daggerlike bristles. Babies were wrapped in a *fascia* and strapped to their mother's backs so women with infants could work."

Gaetano paused, nodded, took a deep breath, and continued. "The *contadini* left their homes in the dark, around four or five in the morning. Whatever the weather, it made no difference. A flowing river of people, they moved like sleepwalkers. To help their legs move, they sometimes sang a sorrowful verse, but mostly they trudged in silence, lost in thought. The men cut wheat. They bent their knees, grabbed several stalks, slashed with a back-and-forth swing of the sharp scythe, and then shoved the shafts into the crook of their arm. They harvested with a rhythm: *swing forward, pull back, cut, cut, cut; swing forward, pull back, cut, cut, cut.* The women, girls, and young boys gathered the wheat by following closely behind, step by step. Families ate lunch together in the fields and continued to work until the sun started to set; going up the hill to Rotondella took longer after a day of hard labor."

Gaetano's voice faded and became an undercurrent in my mental movie. I could imagine the child Carmela working in the fields, following proudly behind her older brother, Giuseppe, wanting to be a help to him. She took the bundle of wheat, when it was not too little and not too big, from her brother's arm. Dividing the stalks into two groups, she rotated her small hands, turning the heads of one cluster of wheat to meet the base of the other, quickly twisting a few stems around and around and binding them together, dropping the sheaf, and reaching for the next armload. Later, she and her older sister, Porzia, would gather them up, place them together in the shape of a giant cross, and heap them on top of one another, forming a small mountain. At the end of the day, her brothers, Giuseppe and Antonio, would arrive with pitchforks to heave the fruits of their labor into a cart. In the afternoon, the young Carmela hacked at the soil to loosen the dirt so she could weed rows of wheat. She raised a pickax above her head, took a deep breath, paused a fraction of a second, and expelled her breath as she accelerated her arms forward, concentrating all her strength on the ground below her feet. The tool pounded into the unyielding clay, and with each assault the clump yielded a little more until it crumpled. She moved down one row and up the next.

Cornelisen's book told of the women of the South who refused to cry out, even during childbirth. Silence was their strength. The women of my history were women of intense determination. Their faces showed *serietá:* seriousness and reliability. Their oath was *omertá,* a code of silence. The women of my history could not show tenderness or tears. The women of my history didn't have the luxury of showing loneliness or joy. The women of my history lived a hopeless life for themselves, but they never stopped fighting to give hope to their children. To survive, they could not give in to fear.

I was beginning to understand how Nonna had become Nonna, a fearless woman who didn't hesitate to protect those she loved; a fearless woman who didn't hesitate to chase down my father with a butcher knife.

Ombretta's voice pulled me back to the present. "Lee-bee, it's time to return to Rotondella and the *commune* for our appointment. *Andiamo.*"

I didn't have to walk or be silent or gather my tools. We climbed into the Alfa Romeo and sped away.

Chapter 17: Via Cervaro

Signor Pancrazio was waiting for us in front of the *commune,* holding a copy of three documents: two birth and one marriage. Ombretta translated the marriage certificate:

> *In the year of 1911, today 23 of September at 10:00 am in the City Hall . . . LaGuardia Vincenzo Gaetano, 25 years old, field worker . . . Perciante Carmela, 22 years old, housewife . . . asked me to join them in marriage. . . . I pronounce the names of the below are joined in marriage . . . Only the witnesses sign because the couple declares to be unable.*

"But, Ombretta." I turned to her with a questioning voice. "This says Nonna was a housewife, not a *contadina.*"

Signor Pancrazio answered, "From what I can piece together, Carmela worked in the fields as a child and young woman, but in time her family became better off than some other families. I discovered they even owned a parcel of land in Caramola, an area at the foot of our mountain and near the river. Owning even a sliver of land was rare in those days, so they must have cultivated their own land in addition to working properties owned by nobles. Her family had animals that, in those years, were considered prized possessions: pigs, chickens, and one mule; having a mule was like having a diamond. It seems they were hardworking and self-respecting people. By the time she married Vincenzo, she did not have to work as a *contadina.*"

"And my nonno's family?"

"They were laborers. Your grandfather, Vincenzo, was a *bracciante,* meaning that he worked with the strength of his arms. Not only did he work the tongues of land assigned to his family but people hired him to do heavy jobs. That's probably how he saved enough money to leave Rotondella. In fact, some members of his family still live here. I called them to ask if they would meet you." He hesitated. "But they declined."

I was shocked and disappointed. "How could they not want to meet me when I've come so far? I'm here for such a short time."

His eyes held sadness. "You don't understand our people. Maybe you never will."

With this, Ombretta stepped in. "Lee-bee, you found what you were searching for in the name of your Carmela. You never knew your nonno. Be satisfied."

Before I could respond, Signor Pancrazio changed the flow of the conversation. "I can show you Carmela's birth home. And, if you're interested, the cemetery."

We climbed into his car and careened downhill toward the wall that surrounded the hill town. He parked on a nearby street, and we followed him down sixteen stone steps and toward a neighborhood called *il Purgatorio,* where Nonna was born. As we were making our way to Via Cervaro, women once again yelled from their windows, *"Chi é?"*

Signor Pancrazio responded with a loud, echoing voice. I couldn't understand what he said, so I looked at Ombretta with raised eyebrows as a way of asking for help. She smiled. "He said that you are an American, but your grandparents were born here in Rotondella. He told these women you belong."

Ombretta and I followed him along the pathway next to the chest-high stone wall that encircled and protected the village. To our right were many abandoned buildings, and to our left, over the wall, was the expansive, harsh, yet mesmerizing landscape leading to the sea. Signor Pancrazio reminded us that Rotondella was called *il balcone dello Ionio,* the balcony of the Ionian, and I could see why. In the distance, I heard a mother calling her son Anthony, *Antó,* with the same dialect words Nonna had called me: *Ven'aqquá.* The church bells of Saint Anthony rang the hour.

Signor Pancrazio stopped in front of Via Cervaro #4. "This is it!" He raised his arm triumphantly. "This is where your nonna was born."

He was pointing to a small gray wooden door, about two inches shorter than my height of five feet six inches and padlocked shut. Built of four wide vertical weather-ravaged planks, the wooden structure was set in the center of a windowless solid stone wall, the color of toasted almonds. There were no windows and, except for the door, there were no openings of any kind.

"Can we go inside?" My voice faltered as I tried to wrap my head around this sight. This was like no home I had ever seen.

"No, it's abandoned," he answered casually. "It's nothing but a cave."

He slung out the word *cave* the way my great-uncles might have slung stacks of cut wheat. He must have registered my shock because he launched into a quick explanation. "You must understand those times. All the *contadini* lived in places like these, holes carved into the mountain. Years ago, it's true that several rich and noble families lived here in the village. They built large palazzi and contributed to our progress for many years. But they left the village to expand their fortunes elsewhere—in Rome or Naples or Milan, or even in larger nearby towns like Policoro. Each year, we have fewer and fewer year-round residents, so we have many deserted places like this, all abandoned. Our young people leave here and move to other regions for jobs."

"What's inside?"

"There's nothing inside," he replied matter-of-factly. "One large, dank, and humid room, the floor made of *pietra grande* stone or hard-packed dirt, which was never dry and always mildewed. It was a cavern excavated out of the stone mountain, with walls of mortar and clay stuck together. There was a door but no windows. The home was fit for animals, not adults, and certainly not for children. But this was all they had."

I turned to Ombretta, my dear guide, to help me understand. She avoided my gaze. This must not have been a surprise to her, probably being another part of Italian history taught to Italian students. I thought about the fields where Nonna worked, the unrelenting labor, and now a home that was nothing more than a cave. Like the pickax that she had used to break and crumble the unyielding clay, I finally yielded to the truth. I finally understood why Nonna didn't want to answer questions about Rotondella. I had thought it was as magical as Oz. Ombretta knew disappointment, not wide-eyed wonder, lay before me, and this explained her reluctance to make things clearer to me. For Nonna, there was humiliation in remembering her early years in Basilicata. This was probably why she shied away from my questions, always changed the subject.

"Let me try to explain," Signor Pancrazio continued more gently. "In those days, there was no electricity, heating, or plumbing—nothing. Try to imagine: They were isolated on top of a mountain. In winter, they slept in their clothes, huddled together for warmth on a straw-filled mattress that was placed on top of a slab of oak that also served as the kitchen table. Sleeping areas were divided by a thin cloth draped from nails pounded into the ceiling, offering privacy of sight but not of sound. Their animals lived and slept inside with them. That's why the door has a smaller opening, for the animals to go in and out. They were their treasures. Someone would have stolen them if they were left in the fields. The pigs slept under the bed and helped to warm the space, especially in winter. Chickens perched on the rafters. The mule huddled in the back corner."

My poor Nonna. No wonder she left for America. I shook my head, as if to make more room for all these facts.

Signor Pancrazio continued, "Mothers scrubbed with all their might to try to keep away illness, especially malaria and typhoid, but it was useless. Illness most often meant death. There were few medicines in the South, and most of those were leftovers sent from the North. These hill towns had only one doctor, often feeble and almost deaf, who had moved to the South, to the *Mezzogiorno,* to pass the last years of his career. He cursed those who were ill because for him it was easier if people died. Try to understand. It was a different time, and your nonna lived a difficult life, as all our people did. Why do you think people emigrated to America? Yes, it took courage, but what were their choices?"

I felt numb and offended at the same time. Numb with so much information and offended by the realization of the squalid conditions in which Nonna had lived. This was like a bad dream, only it was real. More than that, it was my history.

"Nonna never told me these things," I mumbled as I tried to understand all that I was hearing. "I wish I had known."

Ombretta jumped into the conversation. "How could you expect her to tell you these things when you were just a little girl? Lee-bee, you are from another time and another culture. In the United States, you have your history; in Southern Italy, we have ours. In both countries, there have been difficult and desperate times. There is no shame."

"And I'm sure she wanted to forget," Signor Pancrazio chimed in. "She didn't want you to know. She wanted you to be American and to have a new life, a life of prosperity. She wanted you to have a future full of possibility and promise."

Abruptly, I think in an attempt to distract me, Signor Pancrazio announced, "I don't think it's a good idea to go to the cemetery today. It's getting late, and I think you have enough to think about for one day. Tomorrow is another day, when you'll meet Carmela's children. All five were born here: three live nearby and two live in the North. They are good people."

Signor Pancrazio, this gracious man, was trying to help soften the blows, but I had come this far and needed to continue my journey of discovery. "Ombretta and I are leaving the day after tomorrow, so there's little time left. She's given me four days of her life to fulfill this dream. What would have I done without her . . . or you? Thank you both." Then I added, "I'd like to go to the cemetery."

"As you wish . . . " His voice faded in resignation.

Climbing into the car, we drove to the other side of the village. Signor Pancrazio parked, and we walked in silence through a heavy black iron gate and past cypress trees that reminded me of tall and respectful soldiers on guard. A reverential stillness filled my bones.

Stone and marble edifices surrounded us, small shrines and mausoleums made of white polished alabaster, many elaborately carved with pictures of the deceased displayed in oval frames. Names were carved into tombstones or onto the outside walls of small chapels. I saw many Perciantes and even more LaGuardias.

"Which sanctuary is my family's?" I asked Signor Pancrazio. "I know now that these aren't all my relatives, but which ones belong to me?" I was poised with my pen and journal in hand, ready to record the names of my family members, along with dates of births and deaths.

"This is why I didn't want to bring you here." He shook his head sadly. "None of these belong to you. Your family was without sufficient money to afford a burial stone like these," and he swept his arm in a wide arc. "Your family was buried in the common plot where all poor people were placed. Their bodies lay in a public hole for thirty years, after which the bones were dug up, burned to ashes, and put into an *ossario,* a common burial tomb."

Without waiting for my response, he turned and wove his way toward the back of the cemetery. We passed many elegant tombstones and even more holy shrines. I wished Dad or Nonno Vincenzo, with their connections and determination to take care of those they loved, could come back to life and build an edifice for our family.

We stopped in front of a wooden, ramshackle outbuilding that had been built to cover the opening of the *ossario*. I didn't know what to do or say, but this time I didn't look to Ombretta for advice or guidance. I fell to my knees and prayed.

Chapter 18: Goodbye, Rotondella

That night, after a quiet dinner with Ombretta at our hotel in Policoro, I asked to borrow her mobile phone so that I could call my mother. I had ambivalent feelings about all I had learned, and I was hopeful that Mom would be willing to share things she knew about her parents and their lives. Her details would surely help me put some pieces together. I also thought she'd be delighted to learn that Ombretta and I had found her first cousin, who bore the same name as her mother, Carmela Perciante.

Mom answered with a cheery tone, happy to hear from me. I was excited to recount every step in my journey, but I also wanted to be careful not to run up Ombretta's phone bill with a lengthy international call. After a quick hello, I explained that Ombretta and I had not only found Rotondella and birth and marriage certificates, but we had also learned how her parents had lived. Not waiting for her to respond or even acknowledge the situation, I launched immediately into the day's discoveries.

"Mom, you can't believe the poverty. Your mom and dad worked in fields from early morning until late at night, from dawn until dusk. I saw Nonna's birth house—it was a cave! Animals lived in her home; the pig slept under the bed. I couldn't go inside because her house was abandoned and padlocked shut, but . . ."

Like an electric shock, Mom's vitriolic response on the other end of the line stung my ear. "Stop. I don't want to hear this. Stop right now. Do you understand me? I don't know why you had to go back there in the first place, but I don't want to hear about it. Unless you have something positive to say, I'm getting off the phone."

"But Mom, it *is* positive. I met your cousin, the daughter of your Uncle Giuseppe—he named one of his daughters Carmela.

Don't you see how much your mom was loved and remembered? Your parents had amazing courage to leave. I'm learning so much, especially about how the women in our history were strong, brave, and powerful. Don't you see that as positive?"

Silence.

"Mom, are you there? I can't talk for long. I'm using Ombretta's cell phone."

"Yes, I'm here, and I'm not happy about it. Not one bit. Nonna was important to you, but I have different memories. What you're telling me about her life is painful for me to hear, and embarrassing. It's your nature to push, but sometimes you don't know when to stop asking questions or digging for answers."

Now *I* sat silently. How was I to respond?

She continued more emphatically, enunciating each word. "I don't want to know that my parents suffered, or how they suffered. I don't want to hear stories of how my mother carried water on her head, how my parents labored, or about the life they left. You don't need to understand this, but please respect my wishes. We each have memories we want to keep safe and to ourselves. You need to stop. Now, I'm saying goodbye."

The phone line went dead.

After a fitful night's sleep, I awoke to church bells announcing Sunday, Mother's Day, *La Festa della Mamma.* Tomorrow, Ombretta and I were scheduled to return to Florence. I was already feeling anxious because time was slipping away from me. Like a seesaw, I felt caught between satisfaction, knowing I had discovered a great deal about my past, and also disappointment, knowing there was so much more to learn.

At breakfast, I gave Ombretta back her phone and told her about my conversation with my mother. She listened intently but said little. Her sad expression made me realize that she understood my mother's feelings about her parents' lives in Rotondella. Ombretta had more empathy for my mother than I did.

By ten a.m., Ombretta and I were strolling through Policoro's shopping area, where we bought a bouquet of colorful spring flowers for Carmela. Once again, we drove up the winding road leading to Rotondella and into the now familiar streets. Carmela was waiting for us in the kitchen just as Nonna had always been waiting for me.

The elderly woman welcomed us with a warm smile, and I kissed her smooth cheeks. Her eyes brightened as she cradled the flowers and dipped her nose into them to breathe deeply their sweet fragrance. Ombretta explained to me that Carmela had already talked with her children, who would arrive soon, coming directly after Sunday Mass to visit their mom for Mother's Day and to meet us.

This news alerted me that my time with Carmela was shorter than I had anticipated. I was worried that I wouldn't have enough time to get through my list of questions that I wanted to ask her. Dragging a small wooden stool from the far corner of the room, I sat next to Carmela's knee. Ombretta pulled a kitchen chair forward, positioning herself at the apex of our slightly tilted triangle, uniting us and allowing us to communicate.

"I have so many questions," I started sincerely. "May I ask you?"

Placing the flowers on the windowsill, she took my hand gently into hers. Studying her face, I saw deep wrinkles around her eyes and mouth that spoke of both age and hard work, but I also saw an elegant curve to her cheeks and neck that signaled her beauty as a young woman. Her smile held a yes to my question, but she turned toward Ombretta and said something I didn't understand.

"Carmela would like to talk with your mother, Lee-bee," she translated with concern in her voice. She and I both knew this was a risky proposition.

Looking from Ombretta to Carmela, I felt stuck. What should I do? It was only reasonable that Carmela would want to talk to Mom, to ask about their Grandmother Laura and how she died, or to discuss her Aunt Carmela, after whom she was named. This Carmela had many cousins in America, and my mom was her only link. But could I trust that my mother would even talk with Carmela?

Ombretta handed her mobile phone to me, and I made the call. When Mom answered, I greeted her in a light, happy tone of voice, faking a loving mother-daughter relationship and ignoring last night's conversation. I had to bring my mom up to speed quickly, all under the watchful eyes of Carmela.

"Mom, I'm in the home of your first cousin Carmela, the one I told you about. She's sitting here, right next to me. She asked me to call you."

"Yes, I'm listening," came a chilly response.

I ventured into the eye of the storm. "Carmela would like to talk with you."

"It's not possible. How will we communicate?" my mother stammered, feeling caught off guard, the coldness in her voice melting into panic. "I only know dialect, and I'm not sure I even remember much of that. For heaven's sake, Libby, it's been twenty years since Nonna died. Make an excuse for me, but do not pass the phone. Do you hear me? Do *not* pass the phone."

Plastering a smile on my face, I realized I was holding my breath. With wide eyes, I turned to Ombretta for help, but she returned my look with wide eyes of her own. Carmela extended her arms toward me in anticipation, hands open, palms up, ready to receive the phone. Listening to Mom's acerbic voice while looking at Carmela's sweet countenance, I didn't know what to do, but I certainly did not want to disappoint her. I mimed a pleasant response: a smile and a head nod that I'm sure she interpreted as, *Oh, Mom is delighted to talk with you.*

With this nonverbal, unintentional consent, Carmela took the phone out of my hands. I had no time to warn my mother.

Carmela's face brightened as she cradled the phone to her ear. She spoke dialect, and neither Ombretta nor I knew what she was saying, but we could hear the music in her voice, hear the melancholy, and also hear the love.

After a few brief minutes, Carmela ended the conversation with "Ciao, ciao," and she kissed the receiver so my mom would hear. She handed the phone back to me; her eyes welled with tears.

"Mom, this is Libby again. Were you able to understand?"

"Not much," came her soft reply. "No, I couldn't understand all the words, but I didn't need to. Thank you for letting me speak to Carmela. This is difficult for me, and I'm hanging up now. I love you."

*

Sitting next to Carmela, I caressed her hand, lightly tracing the bony fingers and bulging blue veins just as I had done with Nonna. As I was about to begin asking my questions, a cacophony of voices bubbled toward us like water flowing down a sparkling brook. A group was approaching her home, coursing down the same streets Ombretta and I had discovered just yesterday, but this group obviously knew the way; there was no hesitation in their advance and only joy in their sounds. Carmela's children, my cousins, had arrived.

Introductions were made. They were nine in all. Enrico, the only son, handsome in a black-and-white tweed sport coat, perfectly pleated black slacks, and a full head of dark hair, was clearly in charge. His mother had given her approval, but he was the son, the educated one, a business owner, and the family awaited his confirmation. Again, Ombretta was the intermediary, translating nonstop, words flying among eleven Italians and one American. Enrico told Ombretta he recognized the photo from his mother's bedroom, but he took his time to examine the drawing of the family tree, asking Ombretta to explain how we all fit together. After a quick but studious look at me, he kissed me on both cheeks. The sign was clear: I was family.

Marilena and Laura, two of his four sisters, held me and called me *cugina*. Enrico, I learned, was only four days older than me, Marilena was a few years younger, and Laura a few years older. There were two more sisters, Pina and Claudia, who lived in the more northern regions of Lazio and Piedmont. Enrico and Marilena's children, who ranged in ages from eight to fourteen, had accompanied them. I studied each face and memorized names: Enrico was married to Antonietta, and their children were Mimmo and Valeria; Marilena was married to Edgidio, and their children were Gianni and Silvia; Laura had come alone, but had four children: Pietro, Anna, Roberta, and Federico. I looked for resemblances, wanting to see myself in their charcoal eyes, dark hair, thin bodies, high cheekbones, and aquiline noses. These physical similarities held only one part of the answer; our hearts held the other, connecting us as if we had known each other for years. Arms opened, boundaries fell, and love abounded. I was one of them.

My cousins had reserved the day for this reunion. They had planned a tour of the area, a visit to the local museum, an *aperitivo* at Enrico's country house, and a family dinner of homemade ravioli. How could they have known that this was the same dinner—homemade ravioli—that Nonna had made every year to celebrate my birthday?

Ombretta, announcing that everyone was ready to leave, advised me that my questions would have to wait for a return visit. "You'll be back again, Lee-bee." She smiled gently. "You have family now. This is your first visit, but it won't be your last. There will be other times for your questions." Maybe she was right, but I couldn't imagine Rotondella without Ombretta.

As everyone talked at the same time in preparation to leave, Carmela explained that she was a seamstress and had two aprons she'd made: one for me and one for my mother. She wanted to give me something to remember her by, but she already had. She had given me her family.

Kissing Carmela goodbye the Italian way, a kiss on both cheeks, I couldn't resist wrapping my arms around her the American way, hugging her and holding her. I wanted to burn into my memory every touch, every smell, every bone, and every wisp of hair of this Carmela.

She walked me to the front door, holding my hand. Before I left the cocoon of her love and acceptance, she reached up and made the sign of the cross three times on my forehead. In the depth of my soul, I heard Nonna whisper, *I love-a you, Nonnared, from t'e top of you head to t'e bottom of you feet.*

We piled into our cars. Enrico told Ombretta that we should follow him, but she explained that there was one place in Rotondella I still longed to see: the water fountain where Nonna filled barrels and jugs.

"*Certo,*" he responded politely. Like a kind father, he wanted me to understand as much as possible about Rotondella and my history. After a short drive, we parked near the fountain, where he became the guide and Ombretta continued as translator. "The fountain is abandoned now, but at one time it was the center of work: washing laundry as well as fetching fresh water. It took the women at least thirty minutes to walk down the hill and even longer to walk back up. Remember that Rotondella is located about 600 meters high. Climbing from the fountain located at the foot of the village was very tiring for the women. They transported the water in special containers called varril, which they carried on their heads and without any means of transportation. Running water didn't come to homes in Rotondella until the beginning of the 1960s and wasn't completed until 1968."

While Ombretta explained to my cousins why this place held such memories for me, I approached it reverently. To me, it was a sacred place. I felt a deep respect for the memories of the women who had worked here, struggled here, and helped one another survive. The fountain was much smaller than I had expected, twelve feet long and six feet wide at its roundest point, with one silver metal pipe extending two feet from the antique stone wall and spilling water into a half-moon-shaped stone basin. Weeds now sprouted between the cracks, as if to demonstrate their strength of will, much like the women who had once gathered here. I played the mental game of my childhood: I, the young Carmela, filled my jug, the smaller terra-cotta one, shaped like a woman with her arms akimbo, while Mamma Laura filled her wooden barrel and hoisted it onto her head. She took her knitting out of the deep pocket of her apron and started to work as we made our way up the hill. Together, we walked home.

I was lost in my private movie, while my young cousins dipped their hands into the fountain and splashed water on one another, laughing. The past that I cherished had no meaning for them. Like kids everywhere, they were busy with play, with other dreams, dreams that involved the future, not the past.

We climbed back into our cars and sped down the steep incline, away from the heart of Nonna's history, the one she had left in order to build a better future.

I turned my head and looked over my shoulder to bid Rotondella a fond farewell. I was grateful that it had opened its arms and helped me learn about my beloved Nonna. I sealed my memories inside the snow globe, the one of my youth, but this time the scene was not the result of a young child's imagination but of reality. My prayer was that Rotondella would stay the same and wait for me to return.

I never saw my beloved Carmela Perciante again. Two years after my visit, she died. Enrico called Ombretta and, with the heavy heart of an only son, asked her to tell me the news. Eight years later, I did return to Rotondella, but this time without Ombretta. I visited the cemetery to pay my respects to my cousins' mother, Carmela Perciante, the woman who had connected me to my history. She wasn't buried in the *ossario*. Her children had laid her to rest in a magnificent white polished alabaster tomb with her picture displayed in an oval frame.

And as I had done years before, I fell to my knees and prayed.

PITTSBURGH

Chapter 19: Letting Nonna Go

1976

The church was familiar to me. Eight o'clock Mass on Sunday mornings, Nonna and I would sit in our pew, three rows from the altar and on the priest's right. She prayed her rosary and I just prayed. She taught me to pray to God as if I were talking to my best friend. At twenty-five years old, I still did.

I don't remember much of that October day. I was present and not present. I was in church, but I was also feeling Nonna's arms around me, my head tucked softly into her grandmother breasts. I was in church, but I was sitting next to her feet, rubbing my hands against the soft hairs on her muscular legs as we watched *The Lawrence Welk Show*. I was in church, but I was also at her kitchen door as she traced the sign of the cross on my forehead.

Four months earlier, at the age of eighty-seven and while standing on a chair to clean the window above the kitchen sink, she had a stroke. I could imagine her there, wearing her blue-and-white-flowered housedress and her grandmother shoes. She placed her left foot on the seat of a kitchen chair, balanced herself by holding on to the edge of the sink with her right hand, and pushed her left hand onto her raised knee to help hoist herself up. She surveyed the dirt and watermarks, making a tsk-tsk sound, as if reprimanding the window, *How did you get so dirty?* Bending down, she grasped the plastic bottle filled with vinegar and water—she said prepared products like Windex were too *dear*. She sprayed the solution directly onto the glass and started to clean first at the corners, just as she had started at the edges when she spooned sauce over pasta: "You start at t'e outside first, Nonnared, and come inside, or t'e edge get not'-a-ting." She knew how to prepare a plate of pasta; she knew how to clean a window. Louise, the German woman who rented the upstairs apartment, heard a crash and ran down the steps to find Nonna in a heap, disoriented and unable to speak.

Louise called Uncle Tony, and the ambulance arrived and rushed Nonna to Ohio Valley General Hospital. Uncles Tony and Jimmy, Mom, and my aunts took turns keeping vigil. The doctors said Nonna would never recover. Mom wanted to move Nonna into our home, but the doctors recommended a nursing center as the better choice. The stroke had left one side of Nonna's body as dead weight, so she was too heavy for Mom to lift. In addition, Nonna would benefit from twenty-four-hour supervised care. Dad made arrangements at a local nursing home owned by one of his Italian friends. Like Nonno Vincenzo, Dad had connections and took care of those he loved. The words *taking care* meant something special in our family, something big: *You don't have to worry. I have your back. No one can hurt you.*

During this time, I was married, living and teaching in Harrisburg, and Dad and Mom didn't tell me about Nonna's stroke. In August, as soon as my summer school teaching responsibilities ended, I drove home to Pittsburgh, where I was shocked when I learned the news about Nonna. Mom explained that Dad didn't want to disrupt my life: "He just wanted to protect you." But I didn't feel protected. I felt hurt and angry.

Dad was unapologetic. "It was for your own good. There was nothing you could do. Nothing anyone could do. You're married and have a job you love. I want you to enjoy your life. Let Nonna go."

Famous words, I thought—*Let Nonna go*. I wished it were that easy. Three thoughts crossed my mind: One, he was correct that I could do nothing to change Nonna's condition. Two, he was correct that, in the end, I would have to let her go. Three, he was *in*correct that I could do nothing: I could go to her and wait for her, as she had always waited for me. Of course there were other thoughts, but only one mattered: I needed to see her.

He drove me to the nursing home, admonishing me the entire time, "You'll be sorry. You don't want to remember her like this. This is a bad idea. After you see her, you'll tell me I was right. I don't make mistakes, daughter."

He wasn't all wrong. I don't remember all of the day, but the smells will be with me all of my life, that institutional odor of cleaning fluids, medicines, and starched sheets, all floating over the stale scents of food. I also remember Nonna.

She was in an immaculately clean private room with a large window opening onto a pristine green courtyard under the shade of an immense oak tree. The floors of the room were shiny and everything was white: white sheets, white walls, white tables, white plastic cups, and my white-haired nonna. Her olive complexion seemed to be the only color in the room. I stood by the door and watched her as I had watched her when I was a child, but today was different: no glasses, eyes closed, lips not praying, crisp sheets tucked under her chin, and hands out of the bedding with her palms down. Her body looked lost in the white of the bed. I wanted to call out to her and ask her to wake up. I wanted to take her away from this place. I wanted to open my arms and welcome her home.

A chair was next to her bed, and I inched it as close as possible to her. I cradled her right hand in mine, caressed it, and traced with my thumb the blue of her veins and her fragile bones. I thought about her hands and how their movements—their hard work and gentle touches—had always carried messages of her love. I brought her hand to my lips and kissed it.

I needed to be connected to her one last time, to feel her close to me. I needed her to know that I had come. Dad told me that she could still hear, and if she recognized my voice, she could squeeze my hand.

"Nonna, it's Libby. If you know I'm here, squeeze my hand." I pleaded, "Squeeze my hand. Please try. Try hard, Nonna. Do you hear me?" I mumbled these words, each time a little louder, praying that God would give me just one more moment with her.

Tears started to swell in my eyes, and I sniffed hard to hold them back. Maybe she recognized the sound of my tears, a sound familiar to her after all our years together, because it was at this moment when she opened her eyelids just a crack, her eyes filling with tears just like mine. My vision blurred, but I saw her move her lips to try to speak.

"Nonna," I whispered, "squeeze my hand. I'm here."

She squeezed—three times, just as she had made the sign of the cross on my forehead three times. Each tiny push against my palm and fingers was brief, but I felt each one. I knew she was clutching my hand with all her might because this was her way. She loved me from the top of my head to the bottom of my feet. I swear I heard her whisper my name. Just as quickly as she was present, she was absent again. Eyes closed, hand loose, palms down, breath shallow, and she returned to her own world.

Dad and I drove home together in silence; there was nothing more to say.

Nonna died two months later of congestive heart failure. And in the end, Dad would be proven wrong on two counts: one, I would always feel grateful that I went to the nursing home despite his warnings. I would keep that moment by her bedside, her push against my hand, with me forever. She had recognized me. She knew who I was. And two, I would never let her go.

Nonna's funeral Mass was held at Mother of Sorrows Church. Our family gathered to the right side of the large vestibule. I stood behind my mother's slender frame, peering over her right shoulder, and watched the parade of people. Men walked next to their wives, offering their arms for support. Women wept into cloth handkerchiefs with embroidered edges that were either the work of their own hands or the hands of their mothers. Hand-embroidered linens were an obligatory part of their dowry and something that Southern Italian women learned to make during their earliest years.

I remember a sea of black. Women wrapped in black shawls and black coats, and men in black suits and hats. It was that time in Church history when women were required to wear head coverings, and most wore mantillas made of lace, today black. Mine was shaped like a small circle, secured to my hair with a bobby pin. Mom's was a large, intricately laced triangle that covered the crown of her head and hung down the sides of her face, emphasizing her high cheekbones.

Mom kept her head down, weeping. I stood like a block of ice, not crying. I remember the flicker of candles on the main altar, the celestial blue of the Blessed Mother's shrine, and the click and subsequent echo of our heels against the marble floor. I remember the sound of the organ playing "Ave Maria."

My uncles, Dad, brothers, and cousin were the pallbearers who flanked Nonna's casket, guiding it reverently down the center aisle of the church toward the waiting priest and two acolytes. They were the men of our family: soldiers on guard, backs straight and heads high, as if they would protect Nonna with their lives.

As the priest approached the casket with a thurible filled with incense to bless Nonna's body, the pallbearers sat in the pew directly in front of Mom and me. Uncle Jimmy leaned over to whisper to his brother, "What will we do without Mom?" Uncle Tony never moved and never answered, but I saw his thick neck muscles tense as they pressed against the hard starched collar of his white shirt. He was now the head of *la famiglia*.

Some women wept, while others moaned softly. When I was a child, Nonna had explained to me that in Southern Italy wailers attended a person's funeral to mourn the lost soul and to show respect. At some deaths, and especially when the family was rich, she confided, professional wailers were hired. I heard these sounds of sorrow, but I was locked in my own grief, so intense that I could not shed tears as freely as so many others. I refused to believe she was gone.

Following the funeral Mass, cars formed a motorcade as we followed the hearse through the narrow streets of Norwood, driving slowly to St. Mary's Cemetery. Mom rode in the same car as Uncle Tony and Dad. She told me years later, "I sat between them, and they both wept. They never shed a tear in public, but there, in the car as we followed the hearse and next to me, they wept. No one could fathom life without Nonna."

Italian American funerals follow certain traditions. After the rituals of the Mass and the cemetery are completed, all those attending are invited to a reception. Pittsburgh's steel-mill heritage holds true to the ethnic-rich tradition of preparing heaping trays of cookies for weddings and funerals. There was also abundant food, each dish a part of our Southern Italian heritage. Nonna's first question to anyone who entered her home was, "You-a hungree? I make-a you som-a-t'ing t' eat." Food was as central to our living as was our breathing.

The reception was held in Fireman's Hall, across the street from Musmanno's Funeral Home. Mom and her two brothers stood in a receiving line, shook hands, and kissed cheeks. Uncle Tony, the firstborn son, was nearest the door. Mom stood between her brothers; her five-foot, four-inch body diminutive between them. Uncle Jimmy, the youngest and tallest of the three, was last in line. He was the storyteller of the family, and the one who always had a quarter for his young nieces and nephews.

Twelve rectangular tables filled the hall, each covered with a white cloth and surrounded by ten metal folding chairs. Platters of homemade cookies served as centerpieces: biscotti, *pizzelle,* ladyfingers, *piccidat* (called *cucciddati* in Sicily)—cookies filled with ground figs, dates, and walnuts, and *struffoli,* sweet pastry balls dipped in honey. The scent of tomato sauce filled the air with trays of rigatoni, meatballs, and hot sausage with peppers, along with roasted chicken and potatoes, green beans, and, of course, Mancini bread.

Dad and a group of men gathered in the corner opposite the receiving line. Their bodies formed a solid block of black, arms crossed in front of their chests, talking quietly. I approached the circle to feel Dad's strength, but as soon as I got close, the conversation stopped abruptly, and a man with a ruddy complexion and a bulbous nose, smiled benevolently at me while looking at my father and then nodding in my direction. Dad turned, hugged me, kissed the top of my head, and whispered, "Go to your mother. She needs you."

As I turned away, my brother JF touched my arm and asked me if I was OK. I wondered if, like Uncle Tony, all firstborn sons felt responsible for their families. Mom had moved out of the receiving line and was now busy talking with guests and family members, so I wandered around the room, all the while listening closely to what people were saying about Nonna. Initially, the stories and subsequent laughter irritated me, but soon I, too, smiled with fond remembrance.

A group of nonnas, many who had also emigrated from Rotondella, reminisced about the past, when Monday was wash day and soup was the nightly fare; Thursday was spaghetti night; and Friday was ironing day, when they made *pasta fagioli*. Polenta, poured onto a big wooden board and topped with sauce, was part of the weekly rotation, when the family gathered around the kitchen table and whoever ate slowest, ate less. Like Nonna, all these women canned tomatoes, peppers, and made their own grape jelly. When someone in the family was sick, chicken pastina soup cured all ills. For the grandchildren, linguine with ricotta, or sometimes green beans cooked in sauce, topped the menu.

Nonna, like these women, had created a legacy of love, culture, and tradition, all wrapped around food. Sunday dinners were family feasts, with all the aunts, uncles, and cousins gathered around the table. Nonna prepared homemade *frzzul*, gnocchi, *falaoni, braciole,* or roast chicken and potatoes, all accompanied by her red wine. Dandelion salad with oil and vinegar was served last, to help with the digestion. The adults ended with grappa, *amaro,* or coffee spiked with whiskey, which the men called hooch.

Uncle Jimmy regaled a group of men with his stories about the ritual of October winemaking. "Man-oh-man, Mom was tough. After Pops died, she sent me to the produce yard in the Strip District to buy grapes: sixty crates, three crates of red to one white, enough to make the three barrels of red wine that would last a year. She'd give me money, never enough. I had to fight with the guy until I finally walked away, holding a roll of bills so he could see them. I'd yell, *That's too much. Just too damn much. You don't know my mother.* With that, I always got the price she wanted."

I stood back and listened as Uncle Jimmy waved his arms and explained that he and Uncle Tony dumped the grapes into a large round wooden wine press in the basement and secured the lid. A ten-foot-long iron rod threaded through the metal screw at the top of the press and extended equally to each side. He pantomimed how they strained against opposite ends of the bar so the large wooden lid squeezed down onto the grapes and a rosy-colored liquid poured out of the side tube and into a wooden barrel. The men in the group nodded their heads knowingly. They knew the routine; they had done it themselves, most often with their own mothers. Uncle Jimmy's laughter filled the air. "We squeezed those damn grapes till we couldn't budge the bar one more inch. Finally, Tony'd yell, *Mom, what do you want? There's nothing left.*

"She'd shake her hands at him and yell, *Si nu captost!* Jeez, you guys know that Tony could be a hardhead, but he said nothing. We kept pressing until she finally said, *Basta.*"

Foods dominated each conversation. Easters were ushered in with a special bread called *u cuddur*. For the grandchildren, Nonna formed the dough into little baby-doll shapes with a head, torso, arms, and legs, with a hard-boiled egg placed into the center of both the head and belly sections and—presto!—we each had our own *pup c'ddov*, which, in dialect, meant something like an egg baby. The taste of the soft bread was sweet, but not sugar sweet; it was Nonna sweet. Catholics weren't allowed to eat meat on Lenten Fridays, so sometimes Nonna made spaghetti with tuna, but usually she made thick-crusted pizza, the Rotondella way. She topped each circle of dough with her homemade sauce and a little oregano. While the pizza baked, filling the kitchen with aromas of yeast and tomato sauce, she formed the extra dough into long fat cords, attaching the ends to make shapes: circles, figure eights, and braids. She deep-fried these little treats, called *le crispe* in Italian, but Nonna called them *i crisp*. When they cooled enough to eat, we dipped them in sugar and savored every bite.

The floodgates of memory broke loose, and group after group laughed about opening fire hydrants in Norwood to help beat the summer heat, street fairs of hot sausage and peppers stuffed into Mancini submarine rolls, and school picnics at Kennywood Park when the Italian women would lay claim to an entire pavilion so families could lunch together.

But it wasn't all food. There was religion, too, perhaps the most fundamental bond of all. The sacraments of Baptism, First Holy Communion, and Confirmation signified the deepening of one's faith, when families and neighbors gathered together to celebrate. Rosaries, often kept in purses or pockets, were as common as handkerchiefs, and caressing the beads while praying provided comfort in times of trouble. On the feast day of Saint Anthony, the patron saint of Rotondella, the entire community, from young to old, processed to church as the men held high above their heads a statue of San Antò.

That night, after the funeral and reception were over, after people had left and my uncles and their families had said their goodbyes, I sat alone in my childhood bedroom. The house was quiet. Memories of Nonna continued to comfort me. Out of her seven grandchildren, I was the first grandchild to marry. I thought about my wedding, and how Nonna had enjoyed hearing about all the preparations.

"You boy-a-friend is called Teeem, but he is no Cat'olic. *Uffa,* he is Prrres-bee, *ma* I never hear t'is t'ing before, t'is Prrres-bee stuff." Nonna didn't complete the word *Presbyterian* and only rolled her hand near her shoulder as a way of continuing. "And," she added with a concerned face, "he is no from Italy. He is from German. What do you t'ink? I don't know about German and Italy and this Prrres-bee. I don't know about t'is kind-a match."

I could understand her confusion because Mom had told me that immigrant parents demanded their children marry Italian Catholics. Smiling to myself, I tried to ease her concern. "We'll raise the children Catholic. It won't be a problem."

"*Beh.*" She shrugged her shoulders and twisted the edges of her lips down in a kind of what-am-I-supposed-to-say gesture, while looking at me quizzically, as if trying to wrap her head around this. She touched my cheek and continued, *"Ma,* I lik-a him and I lov-a you."

No one expected her to come to the church, because she was eighty-four and stubbornly refused to leave her home except to go to the grocery store. Her typical response to any invitation was, "No, I stay home. You go. Hav-a fun." But Nonna was determined to come to my wedding, so Uncle Jimmy accompanied her to Heinz Chapel at the University of Pittsburgh, where my older brother, her firstborn grandson, escorted her to her seat. She held on to his arm and walked next to him like the matriarch she was: head up, back straight, eyes forward. When I walked down the aisle with Dad, I saw her standing at the end of the pew and holding herself steady by grasping the carved wooden bench in front of her. She looked at me, her eyes filled with tears. I stopped, raised my veil, and kissed her. She touched my face with her fingertips, and our eyes met in love. I felt her saying, *Ti voglio molto bene, carissima; I want the world to give you the best, and if I could give you the world, I would.*

Nonna surprised us all by coming to the reception, where two receiving lines formed: one formal, in front of the bridal party, and the other informal, in front of Nonna. All those who knew her—and some who didn't—wanted to say hello and offer their respect.

In Southern Italy, there is a traditional folk dance often performed at weddings called the tarantella. This dance captivated my imagination, and even as a child, I badgered Nonna to dance with me in her kitchen as I sang out, "Tata dada, tata dada, tatadadata." She loved me, so she would smile and move a few quick and rhythmic steps, surprisingly light on her feet for a grandmother, stepping this way and that, until she collapsed into a chair, laughing and telling me that she didn't remember any more of "t'is kind'a dance." For months prior to my wedding, I begged her to dance the tarantella with me at the reception. "No," she huffed flatly. "You are crazy. I can no dance. No one knows t'is dance. Go away wit' t'is idea."

However, Mom had instructed the bandleader to make sure his group knew how to play the tarantella. Near the end of the cocktail hour and before dinner, Nonna announced she was ready to leave. Immediately, my mother cued the bandleader, and the music of the tarantella filled the room. It was then that a small miracle happened. For a moment, Nonna sat quietly. Then she looked up and met my eyes, nodded her head, and reached out her right hand toward me, wiggling her fingers downward and toward her in a kind of beckoning motion.

She stood, took two steps toward me, and began to dance. She clapped her hands and twirled first to the right, then to the left, all the while holding up the front edges of her dress just a tiny bit by bending her wrists and tilting her hands up toward the ceiling. I followed her every movement while guests formed a circle around us. Out of her pocket, Nonna took a crisp white handkerchief decorated by her own elaborately hand-crocheted work, one she had embroidered over sixty years ago as part of her dowry. She held on to one end and I held on to the other. We raised our arms in the air, connected by the treasured memory of her own wedding. Around and around we danced to our right with a one-two-three, one-two-three step. Then we changed hands, holding on to her cloth again, lifted our left hands, and danced around and around in the opposite direction. She never smiled. I could have sworn she was in Rotondella, dancing with Vincenzo.

Just as quickly as she had signaled for me to dance with her, she nodded again. She was done. She kissed both my cheeks and made the sign of the cross on my forehead, mumbling something in dialect. Tim appeared at her side, and she kissed him too. Then, she turned to Uncle Jimmy: "Now, I go home." She walked away with a light step and a smile.

We all continued as she had shown us. We raised our hands together and danced the tarantella. I danced with my husband, imagining that I, too, was in Rotondella.

But now Nonna was dead, and I was in my parents' home, far from Rotondella. Dad was asleep and Mom, still awake, sat at the kitchen table. I was leaving early the next morning because I had to get back to my school responsibilities, but I wanted to talk with Mom. I had something to ask her.

She looked depleted, as if she were a million miles away, with a cup of coffee, probably ice-cold, in front of her. I considered leaving her alone, but as was my nature, I plowed ahead. There were three things, I told her, that I would like to have to remember Nonna. At first, my mother looked at me blankly. I waited until she focused her eyes on me and smiled faintly. When I knew she was listening, I began.

First, Nonna had told me that when she died she wanted me to have the Murano glasses that I had brought from Venice. I felt sure no one else wanted them, so I moved on quickly.

Second, Nonna had promised me her hand-crocheted tablecloth, the large one for a table setting of twelve persons, the one she had made in Rotondella as part of her dowry. She had carried it on her voyage to America. I knew the tablecloth was a masterpiece, one that had required hundreds of hours of labor. I reminded Mom that when I was a child, Nonna had taught me how to crochet, and I assured her that I certainly understood that the tablecloth was a work of art and something to be treasured.

Then, pausing only a moment, I pushed forward. "The only other thing I really hope for, if it's OK with you and your brothers, is the picture of Nonno, your grandmother, and Nonna holding you when you were little. You know, the photo that hung on Nonna's wall above the couch in her living room? You might want the picture because you're in it, and I understand, but the Murano glasses were something I gave her and the tablecloth was something she promised me. If I could have these three things, I'd be so very grateful."

Mom looked at me with sad eyes and said nothing. I thought her silence was because she might be thinking I was greedy. Her mother had just been buried and her selfish daughter was already asking for things.

Maybe someone else wanted Nonna's wedding ring? I didn't know why I thought about the ring, but I did. I had worn it proudly ever since the day Nonna gave it to me, so I couldn't imagine that this was a problem. Maybe someone else wanted the tablecloth? Who even knew the value of her work? My mother's depressed look and her lack of a response disappointed me, but I feared I had disappointed her. I could understand if I had.

Mom shook her head slowly and looked toward the ceiling as if trying to find the answer there. I knew she was lost in her own grief, so I thought, *OK, I'll just wait.* There was no rush. Impulsive by nature, I rarely chose the right time to bring up an issue. I leaned over, kissed the top of her head, and turned to leave the room. We could talk later, during a less emotional and heartbreaking time.

She stopped me by taking my hand in hers. "Everything's gone. The tablecloth, the Murano glasses—all gone." She covered her face with her hands and wept.

"How can that be? It's not possible." I felt trapped between wanting to comfort her and wanting to rage at this violation.

"We don't know what happened. When Tony and Jimmy went to her house after her stroke, everything of value was gone." She took a deep breath and attempted to regain her composure. "There was no sign of forced entry. Maybe," she stammered, "I forgot to lock the door. Maybe my brothers. We just don't know. The photograph is still there. I'll talk with Tony and Jimmy. I'll ask if you can have it. If you can't have the original, we'll make a copy for you. I'm sorry."

I started to protest, but she lifted her palm to stop me. Bowing her head as if in prayer, she sighed. "Let it go, Libby. You need to learn to let things go."

Dad had told me to let Nonna go. And now my mother had said the same words. Maybe that's what my life was to be about: learning to let go. Maybe the lesson was that I couldn't hang on to things or people, regardless of how much I loved them. I touched Nonna's ring. I didn't have to let that go.

Nonna was gone, and many of her treasures were gone too. I had no control over any of it and had no choice but to accept so many losses. Silently, I returned to a bedroom still littered with stuffed animals I had accumulated as a child, closed the door, and wept.

Chapter 20: Laura's Letting Go

2012

In November, the business of dying ruled each day. Mom's life was confined to a private room with an adjoining bathroom in the Masonic Village Nursing Home, a clean, comfortable, and warm space where she would spend her remaining days.

End-of-life issues abounded as she swung between telling me she loved me and giving me orders. Fragile in some ways and like a street fighter in others, she fought dying but prepared for its inevitability.

"I want you to call Musmanno's Funeral Home and ask about cremation."

"What do you want me to ask, Mom?"

"Oh, ask him factual information like cost . . . Oh, never mind, get your journal. I'll dictate a list of questions."

I propped her swollen feet on top of another cushion, hoping that the additional elevation would help drain the fluid. Even though the nurses were plying her with Lasix, a diuretic, the edema was winning the battle as it continued its insidious assault, beginning in her feet, creeping into her ankles, and invading her calves. When I pushed into it, the pitting lasted for a count of three. I felt powerless against this encroaching enemy.

That afternoon, when I returned to the nursing home and Mom, I announced that I had made the call as she had asked.

"What did you find out?" she responded with false lightness in her voice, seemingly curious to hear.

"I talked with Anthony, the owner. He said *you* called him—three months ago—and you two had a lovely conversation. In fact, you told him that you went to high school with his father. He told me not to worry because he already knew exactly what you wanted."

She smiled a half smile, as if pleased with herself. Those eyes of hers avoided my accusing gaze, much like a child who had been caught with her hand in the cookie jar.

"OK. That's reassuring to know. Now, I have something else I want to ask you," she announced, taking charge again. I nodded, not surprised.

"When I pass, will you clean out my apartment? I don't want anyone else going through my personal things. I'd like my daughter to do it."

As if I had been knighted by the queen, I felt proud and honored.

"Sure, Mom. Of course."

Later that evening, before I left the nursing home, she directed me: "Go into my bedroom. In the bottom right drawer of my long dresser, you'll find a brown, rectangular leather box. It's the only container in the drawer. Don't open it. Just bring it to me."

The next morning, I handed her the case, four-inches wide and eight-inches long. I had followed her instructions and had not opened it. She held it like a prayer book, fingering the outside edges, lost in her thoughts. She placed it on her belly and patted the edge of the bed for me to sit.

"I was married before I married your father."

I did know this. She had had to tell me about it five years earlier. I was applying for Italian citizenship and, searching in the Allegheny County records for my parents' marriage certificate, I found nothing. When I asked her about this, she looked as if I had slapped her, then turned away. Only after several minutes of silence did she tell me to check marriage records in Johnstown, Pennsylvania, where a justice of the peace had married my parents.

My mother explained it to me. "I hated my life in my parents' house, so I married my boyfriend, Brian. We eloped to West Virginia. After I met and fell in love with your dad, Brian and I divorced."

She and my dad had kept this secret for over sixty years. I was both blindsided and stunned. True to my nature, I had dug into my own research and found the marriage and divorce records that I needed. I also discovered that divorcing in the mid-40s was considered scandalous, especially in an Italian-Catholic family. At that time, the divorce rate among Italian-Catholics was only 2 percent.

She wrote to Brian and demanded a divorce. When he returned from the service, he fell to his knees, wept, and begged her to stay. But she turned her back and walked away. When Carmela discovered what Mom had done, she beat her to the ground. My mother told me, "No one, before or after, ever beat me so ferociously."

Her divorce from Brian was finalized in July 1946, and one month later she and Dad had married. When I confronted her with this information, she explained, again reluctantly. "Brian was sweet and kind, but I could walk all over him. I couldn't walk over Ted. He was the one I wanted."

Now she spoke of Brian again and held the box out to me. "Brian gave this to me as a wedding gift. I haven't opened this case for years. I'd like you to open it."

She was asking me to open the gift that Brian had given her, something she had kept hidden from everyone, including my dad. I furrowed my eyebrows and dipped my chin as if to say, *Are you sure?* She responded by pushing lightly on my arm, her eyes on the box. The closure was stiff against my fingers, as if resisting the invasion. I slid my thumb inside and pried it open.

Pearls, the color of eggshell, lay nestled on a brown felt bed.

"You kept these buried in your drawer all these years, Mom," my voice held the question.

"Yes, I don't know why. I couldn't part with them."

I lifted them out and cradled them in my palm. I felt as if I was holding Brian's very heart. Then I held the pearls by the clasp and reached my hand toward her, thinking she would take the necklace, but she didn't move. Suddenly, the ancient string broke, the pearls tumbling onto the bed, cascading over the edge and bouncing onto the floor. I gasped, lunging after them and trying desperately to gather them together, as if to gather together their love. Many pearls evaded my grasp, just as my mom had evaded me all her life. They ran from me just as I had run from my mother all my life.

Mom gripped my shoulder and said firmly, "Let them go. It's been a long time. They don't matter anymore."

She never mentioned the pearls again, but she wound her way back to my dad. "Did you know that I met your father at my mom's kitchen table?"

I thought back to all the meals Nonna and I had shared at her kitchen table, but I never considered that my mother and father could have had a life there before me.

Her eyes grew distant. "It was during World War II. Brian shipped out just six months after our marriage, so I returned to my mother's house. Your dad had been medically discharged after suffering several bouts of malaria while fighting on Guadalcanal. He moved to Pittsburgh to work and was living in Woodsey's boardinghouse across the street. Jimmy played pickup basketball games with Ted and often invited him to dinners at our house. I knew from the first moment I met him that he was a man who would make something of himself.

"Of course, I worked during those years. With most men away and fighting in the War, many women had what we called men's jobs. I worked for Maison Felix Beauty School, where I single-handedly opened six schools, supervised build-out, hired teachers, and enrolled more than one hundred students. I had the necessary spunk and savvy to make things happen.

"Johnstown was the last school I opened. Ted had taken a job there at a successful photography studio to learn everything he could. I moved into his hotel room. The problem was that I was married."

After her divorce from Brian and her marriage to Dad, she became pregnant and, soon after, she and Ted moved back to Pittsburgh. There, they started their own business from the ground up. "I was the one who knew how to start a business and how to run one—I had done it. I was a crackerjack!"

Then, in a more sober tone, she continued. "Ted learned from me, became dynamite, and a great businessman. When he didn't need me anymore, he kicked me out of the company. I was crushed. We had many rocky years. He could be faithful for a time and then he couldn't. We fought. Religion became my salvation. I became a prayer warrior, and God filled the void in my life."

Her narrative wound down. I listened to the hum of the oxygen machine and the scratching of my pen on the pages of my journal. Mom's eyes closed, and I thought she was asleep until I heard her say, "Ted was the love of my life and I never stopped loving him. He wasn't all that I wanted or all that I needed, but he was mine, and I miss him."

People in the nursing home loved Mom, and she had many visitors, including doctors, nurses, the director, and the chaplain. Her care and medication were closely monitored, but one morning, when I arrived, she looked at me with a blank expression, and her tongue seemed thick as she tried to speak. She seemed out of it, confused, and languid, as if she had been heavily sedated during the night. This was deeply disconcerting because Mom was always alert, her vocabulary often more robust than mine. I asked the nurses, who dutifully checked their charts, and they assured me that Mom had been given her usual dosage of sleeping medication. Not satisfied with their responses, I felt an urgent need to protect Mom—from what I wasn't sure—but I decided to sleep in her room to verify that she was well-supervised during the graveyard shift.

At ten thirty that night, when I returned to her room after changing into a comfortable sweat suit, she was already fast asleep. I curled onto a leather cushioned chair that was next to her bed, draped a blanket over my body, and rested my head on a pillow. Sometime around three a.m., I heard her.

"What are you doing sleeping in the chair?" Her voice was shrill.

"I told you, Mom, that I was going to sleep here tonight to make sure you're OK. It's fine. Go back to sleep."

In a confused haze, she tried to get out of the bed. Immediately, I sprang up from the chair and sat next to her, holding her hand and caressing her shoulder. "Lie back down, Mom. I'm right here."

She glared at me. "Listen, young lady. I don't know why you're so stubborn. You can't sleep in a chair. I refuse to sleep at all unless you sleep here with me. There's enough room. Sleep right next to me in this bed or go home."

The commanding one was still calling the shots. I gave in willingly. "OK. Move over."

She scooted a bit to her right and I lay next to her.

"See, now it's like a slumber party." Her voice was calm again. "Aren't you more comfortable in bed with me?" She held my hand and we fell asleep.

At some point later, while it was still dark, the room lit dimly only by the light from the hallway, she awakened again, more alert this time.

"Do you remember," her voice nudging me out of sleep and into consciousness, "when Jeff was a baby and he almost died?"

I had no idea what initiated this bout of melancholy remembrance. We had both been asleep, and maybe she had been dreaming about Jeff. I decided to go along. "Yes, Mom. I remember."

"He was only three months old and in Pittsburgh's Children's Hospital. You were completing research for your doctoral dissertation at the University of Pittsburgh and you were busy, so I backed you up at the hospital and took care of him. It was such a joy for me. While he slept, I held that little body on my chest for hours. I never wanted to let him go, or let him sleep alone in the cold bed. I prayed all day long, and I'd lift his little arms into the air and say *even little children will praise the Lord.* Then, when he got better, you both lived with us, with Dad and me, for three months while you finished your dissertation. Remember? When you were at the University teaching or downstairs writing your thesis, I had Jeff upstairs and all to myself. I put him on a blanket and dragged him from room to room while I cleaned and cooked. I never left him alone, and we talked all day together. He squealed and I told him stories. Then, when Jeremy was born, I came to your house and took care of Jeff. He was only twenty months old, but we were buddies and went everywhere together. One day, a basket of artificial flowers was delivered to the house, and I hung it from the kitchen lighting fixture.

"*What do you think, Jeff? How does it look?*"

"That little squirt stared up at me and said, *Look dumb.* And he was right!"

She fell silent, and I thought she had gone back to sleep, but moments later, she began again. "And Jeremy. When his appendix ruptured, I came and took care of your family. He was only nine years old and in Washington, DC's Children's Hospital for a whole month. When he came home, I spoiled him and jumped to his every need. I set my alarm for three a.m., so I could give him his medicine. You were working at Calverton and I didn't want you to wake up, but I knew he needed his medication during the night. I hugged him every chance I got and cooked all his favorite foods to fatten him up after his surgery; he had lost so much weight. I even bought him a new mattress, a softer one, so he could rest more comfortably.

"You see," she said, and there was a hesitating quality, "I wasn't a good mother to you, but I was a good grandmother to your children."

My voice, filled with tears, whispered back, "Mom, you were a great grandmother. My boys cherish you. I can never thank you enough. When I needed help, you were the only one who came."

Silence drifted through the darkness, punctuated by the whining of the oxygen machine and the squeaking sneakers of the medical staff as they passed in the hallway.

Her voice continued, "Can you forgive me for not loving you, for not knowing how to love or protect you?"

She lay quietly next to me, her eyes closed, waiting for me to respond. Forgiveness had started to take shape, but I was too stubborn, or maybe the wounds were embedded too deeply in the very muscles of my heart. I knew that a part of me had forgiven her, while another part continued to nurse the pain. On the other hand, she needed sleep, and she deserved peace.

"Yes, Mom, I forgive you."

"Thank you." She opened her eyes and looked directly into mine. And she saw what I didn't say.

Mom's physical condition shifted daily, sometimes hourly. There were times when she was alert and focused, demanding to exercise with the physical therapist or mustering all her strength to shuffle independently on her walker into the bathroom, but there were other times when she was afraid and confused. She rarely spoke about these moments of weakness, but I remember one event clearly.

"I'm afraid I'm not as sharp as I used to be. Don't you agree? You see it, don't you?"

"No, Mom. You're fine. At ninety-one years old, you remember more than I do."

"Test me. Test me on numbers. Ask me a phone number and see if I remember it correctly."

"Mom, I don't even know any phone numbers." I laughed kindly. "If it weren't for my mobile phone, I wouldn't be able to call anyone."

She stretched uncomfortably, reaching into the dressing table drawer next to her bed. She pulled out a small white box onto which she had scribbled something.

"I tested myself." She looked at me seriously, eyes flashing with rebellion. "This afternoon while I was watching television, there was a commercial with a phone number listed. I studied it as hard as I could, waited one minute, and then wrote it down from memory. It's here—I wrote it here. You look at the number while I'll tell you the digits. Then tell me if I'm correct."

Touching her left foot, I walked toward her while my hand traced the dips and valleys of the sheet over her thin and ravaged body. I allowed myself to feel the swelling in the foot, the ankle, and the lower part of her calf, the bony knee, her fleshy thigh. On her hip—broken twice—I could feel the edges of bone.

She handed me both the box and her glasses. She and I shared the same reading glasses, 1.75 strength, bought at the Dollar Store.

I slid the glasses onto my face, while her eyes, dark like the midnight sky, stared back at me. What did I see there? Fear. I saw fear because I think she already knew the answer to her test, but I also saw hope and trust: hope that maybe she could remember correctly and trust that if she couldn't, I would keep her secret.

I looked at the box onto which she had written the numerals in pen. There were only five digits, not seven, and only three were legible.

"Mom, I have a better idea. Instead of you remembering something from some stupid commercial, how about if you tell me the number for Mancini Bakery?"

With a half smile of knowing what I was doing, she recited it with ease.

*

When the chill of mid-November hit, I needed to return to my home in Italy. When I had arrived in Pittsburgh to take care of Mom, it was summer, so I hadn't packed coats, boots, or sweaters. Although I kept a stash of clothes in the second bedroom of Mom's apartment, the bulk of my winter clothes were still in Florence. I talked with both Dr. O'Donnell and the hospice nurse about being away for a week, and they both gave me their blessing. The kind doctor advised, "Just let her know when you'll return. That way, she'll know that you'll be back and have peace about your leaving."

Once I arrived in Florence, I called Mom every day on her mobile phone. Most days she answered, but when she didn't—whether because she hadn't heard the phone ring, was busy with visitors, or was having physical therapy—I would call the nurse's station and leave a message for her that I would call again the next day. On Thanksgiving morning, she answered happily. "I can talk with you forever because I can ramble and relax. I don't have to be anyone or work at anything talking with you." Then she asked, "Have you met anyone yet?"

I wasn't surprised by this question because on several occasions during the last ten years, she had told me that she was praying for my spiritual mate and intended not to pass until I married someone. She was comforted knowing that Tim and I were still close and working together for the good of our sons, but she wanted me to be taken care of by someone. Even if I didn't agree with her, it didn't matter.

"No, Mom. No one yet."

"I think you're afraid and that's why you haven't met anyone," she said. I could almost see her, my tiny mother lying in bed and attached to oxygen, nodding with assurance that she was correct. At ninety-one, she was still smart. Maybe she couldn't remember phone numbers with ease, but she was no one's fool.

"You're right, Mom. I am afraid, and I'm not sure when it will change."

"You know," she began another conversation. "I'm becoming acclimated to getting along without you. Do you know that?"

"That makes me sad, Mom."

"No, I didn't tell you to make you sad. I told you to set you free."

Tears blurred my vision as I looked out the window of my apartment to the deep green of the magnolia trees against the blue Tuscan sky. She continued, "I admire you: your stability, your strength, your ability to love. You have so much love to give. I wish I had seen those gifts when you were a little girl. But I see them now."

I said nothing but knew in my soul how I had hungered all my life to hear these very words. I heard them now and I was grateful.

"Everyone asks about you. Do you know that?" she reported, her voice lilting upward again. "They say we look alike," and in my mind's eye, I could see her smile. "I don't see the resemblance, but it makes me happy to hear it."

Then, I heard something over the phone line, like a sigh that holds a million hurts. Her words turned inward.

"I'm tired. I'm so, so tired. Wouldn't it be nice if I could go home?"

"Mom, are you ready to go home?" My question held both sadness and the knowledge that we were on the final descent.

Three words came back to me, each one spoken in a quieter and more diminished tone.

"Yes.

"Yes.

"Yes."

That night at eight thirty Italian time, I received another call, but this one was from Mom's hospice nurse, "I'm calling to tell you that your mom will die in the next two or three days."

As if a gun had exploded close to my ear, my head reverberated, and I had to shut my eyes to regain my balance. Sure, I knew death was inevitable, but another part of me wanted to believe it would never come.

"I hear what you're saying, but I just talked with her earlier today and she sounded fine. Give me a few minutes to wrap my head around this. I'll call you back."

The next phone call I made was to Mom's doctor. He was sympathetic but hadn't yet heard from the nursing home that Mom was failing. He promised to check on her as soon as possible. I waited.

Mom's life was coming to a close. Nothing had changed, except maybe everything had changed. She was struggling to remain in control but, sadly, control wasn't her call anymore.

When I was a child, I created my own imaginary glittering worlds, like soap bubbles that kids blow into the air; they float, they astound, they sparkle and wobble, they change shapes and glisten like jewels. When I was a child, I dunked my wand into the fantasy that I created: Dad was Robert Young, and Mom was Jane Wyatt in *Father Knows Best*, and we were the happy family of five: the Fabulous Five. Blowing bubbles of my invention, I comforted myself by magically transforming the reality that was my life into glistening and shimmering orbs.

Another phone call, the one for which I had been waiting. "I've checked your mom. She's pallid, frail, and has a moist cough. I think we're looking at a week, maybe two."

"Should I come home?"

"Yes."

And now I prayed that the fragile sphere of Mom's life would last long enough for me to get back to her.

When I walked into her room, tired from the transatlantic flight, her face was radiant and her eyes danced. "Ahh," she squealed with delight, "I heard you were coming. You know I'm glad to see you and you know I love you dearly . . . " I heard in her voice a hesitation and I knew a *but* was coming.

A pause. A change in expression, as if to lecture me, raising her right eyebrow to drive home her next words, *"But* you made a *big* mistake coming home. I'm fine."

"You're just as beautiful as ever, Mom." My words were the music I thought she needed to hear. "I got a call saying you were dying and I should come home."

"Let's not talk about me dying . . . " She contorted her face, shaking her head back and forth, as if trying to erase the thought. "You're here now and that's all that matters. You'll be proud of me when you see how much better I'm doing. I'm really trying."

Uncharacteristically, she didn't ask me about my flight, critique my hair, or wonder if I was hungry. She did, however, want to know how long I was staying. Even on her deathbed, she was lucid. She remembered that in early October I had purchased tickets for both my sons to fly together to Italy so we could celebrate an early Christmas in Florence.

"You can't stay long, you know," she continued in a let-me-tell-you-what-to-do voice. "You've already planned this trip with the boys, and they've both made time in their work schedules to come. This won't happen again, just the three of you in Italy. When are they leaving?"

"All three of us are scheduled to fly out of New York on December 4, but that's in ten days. Let's see what happens, Mom. Nothing is carved in stone."

"Umm," her mouth set into one straight line, "we'll see about that."

During the following days, I observed her closely. She had moments of brightness and joy, but more often, the moments were clouded over by what she called "the fog." I wasn't sure if these episodes indicated her failing or if they were caused by medication, pain pills, or the tiring effects of visiting with people. I felt confused, so I asked our kindly Dr. O'Donnell.

"She seems better, brighter. Her feet and calves are still swollen, but she's eating. What am I missing?"

"She rallies when you're around," he said gently. "Haven't you noticed?"

Each night, Mom and I had a routine we followed: I helped her into the wheelchair and rolled her into the bathroom where she, independently and with great pride, brushed and flossed her teeth, washed her face, always following with a moisturizer applied with an upward hand movement, carefully patting the skin under her eyes. "You never want to pull the delicate skin under your eyes," she instructed in an experienced tone of voice. Her body, once smooth and moist, was now like flaking onionskin, so I rubbed her with scented lotion, especially her back.

But this night, instead of following our prescribed steps, she had other plans.

"Now that you're here, I'm going to show you how much progress I've made. I'm going to stand up by myself and then, once I'm standing, you can help me sit in the wheelchair and push me into the bathroom."

She cocked her head to the side and looked at me with determination, as if to remind me who was in charge, dropped her chin, and nodded once. Whispering like a wounded soldier, she instructed me, "Now, you stand close to me, but don't touch me. Don't . . . touch . . . me." She wagged her index finger into the air while emphasizing each of the last three words.

She placed her open hands to her sides, next to her hips, and onto the bed for leverage, pushing with all her might and trying to rise up into a standing position. Nothing happened. Next, she grabbed onto the top bar of her walker, pulling her body forward and straining her face with effort. Again, nothing. Finally, she gritted her teeth while holding on to the lower rail of her walker, tugging and straining her tiny body upward. Nothing.

This was the woman who once beat me.

"You know I have fears," she admitted, continuing to sit in the same spot on the edge of the bed, breathing hard, depleted from her attempts to stand. "But I have courage too. When you were gone, I was sitting right here, in this exact same space, and I tried to reach for the wheelchair so I could take myself into the bathroom, all by myself. I stretched with all my might, like this . . . ." And she showed me, as a child might show a parent, how she reached, so far, almost touching. "I was within inches, but I couldn't quite make it, so I decided not to take the chance. You see, I had the courage to try, but I was afraid I'd fall."

"I'm glad you tried, Mom, but I'm more glad you didn't fall."

"But don't you understand?" she pleaded with me. "When I yell at you, it's because I'm afraid of something. I know I've hurt you, and I'm sure I still do. I have many regrets, but most of what I did wrong, I did when I was afraid. I'm still learning about myself, don't you see? It takes a lifetime to learn how to live."

*

Two days before my sons and I were scheduled to return to Italy, Mom was in rare form. What I didn't understand then, but see clearly now, is that she was struggling to hold on to her independence, even at death's door.

"Before you leave, I need you to schedule three medical appointments for me: an eye appointment, a podiatrist appointment, and a dental appointment. My teeth haven't been cleaned for quite some time and I don't want anything to happen to them. I certainly don't want partials."

Of course I said I would do as she asked, but her insistence for me to complete this list of events that would be scheduled within the upcoming weeks or maybe month confused me. When Dr. O'Donnell came to visit, and after he had checked Mom, I accompanied him into the hallway to talk with him privately outside the door.

"Doc, I have plans to leave for Italy with both my sons, but I'll return to Pittsburgh in ten days. Mom is standing at the sink, washing her face and brushing her teeth. She told me today she wants to start physical therapy again, and even asked me to coordinate three medical appointments with specialists. Having my sons with me in Italy would be a dream come true, but I don't want to leave if anything will happen to her while I'm gone. What do you think? Should I leave or not?"

Looking over the top of his glasses, his eyes filled with deep gentleness. "Why don't you ask her?"

When I returned to her room, she said, "What did Dr. O'Donnell say?"

"He said it's a slow process."

"What's a slow process?" she asked me with her eyes closed.

"This dying thing."

She nodded her head up and down slowly. Her body was tiny and lost in the white of the sheets, hardly a bump. If you didn't know she was there, you might think the bed was empty. She patted the bed beside her hip—her way of signaling for me to sit beside her. I could feel in my bones what she wanted to tell me.

As I settled next to her, she cradled my hands. Her body felt warm; her hands were like ice. Riveting her black eyes into mine, she waited until she was satisfied that I was truly present. When she was ready, her voice filled with conviction as she told me, "I want you to go. This could be a once-in-a-lifetime trip when you have both sons with you. Just the three of you. If something happens to me while you're gone, please be happy for me. I want to pass and go home. I'm so tired. I can't continue to live like this."

I nodded. I knew that her dying wasn't the hardest part. The hardest part would be never seeing her again, never hearing her voice again, and never seeing those eyes that I had once feared and now loved.

She reached up her hand and touched my face, trying to wipe away my tears. The same gesture as Nonna.

"And don't cry," she said soberly. In these words, I heard her need, the need that said, *Please don't cry. I can't stay strong if you cry.*

"I won't cry, Mom. I won't."

"Good," she said tenderly.

"But I miss you already."

The day before my leaving, she wanted to get out of the bed. "Help me get into the wheelchair. I'd like to sit by the window with you."

I positioned her out of the direct rays of the sun but facing the window, with a clear view of the Pennsylvania landscape of barren winter trees and tall evergreens. I sat on the window seat across from her. She smiled at me. Her face looked absolutely flawless, almost beatific and radiant.

Knowing I was leaving soon, I wanted to make sure that I had done everything possible for her. I needed to leave knowing that I had done my best until the very end. "Is there anything you need from me before I go? Is there anything I can do, say, get for you? Anything at all?"

"Yes. I have a question for you."

I waited. My mother, this little sparrow of a woman, seventy-eight pounds and ninety-one years old, stared at me as if she were looking into my soul. The room was silent except for the hum of the oxygen machine. The window was open, and I felt a slight warm breeze against the back of my neck.

"Are you *sure* you forgive me?"

This was the third time she'd asked me. The first was when she was headed into surgery. The second was when we spent the night together, during our slumber party. This was the third time, and I knew it was the last. There would be no more conversations about this.

"Yes, Mom." Immediately and without hesitation, the words welled up from inside me. "I forgive you."

She recognized it as truth. "Thank you." The edges of her lips lifted into a smile, and then, as though this required too much energy, she closed her eyes, took a deep breath, and fell into a gentle quiet, as if in prayer. I closed my eyes, too, and felt an entirely new calm in my spirit, one I had never felt before. Not ever.

"You know I'm glad we talked about all these things," Mom started again, her eyes still closed. "About my life, and especially all my memories about my own mother. She hurt me. I never felt her love, only her beatings, her abandoning me, her preferring anyone else's company to mine. I forgave my mother once before, years ago, but since we've been talking and I've been remembering, I've forgiven her again. Just as you've now forgiven me."

I waited for her to continue, knowing she had more to say. She opened her eyes and looked out the window at the rolling Pennsylvania hills, the ones she had known all her life. Her eyes faded and she grew distant, as if she were looking backward, remembering another time.

"When Nonna was in the nursing home after her stroke, she was unresponsive; she couldn't speak or move. At that time, I was in a prayer group, and one of my prayer partners knew I was carrying tremendous anger and resentment against my mother. My friend told me, 'You have to forgive her so she can die and you can live in God's peace.' I prayed about it for a long time and decided I would try. I drove to the nursing home early one evening, sat next to Mom, and held her hand. I caressed her cheek, told her I forgave her, and that I understood how hard life had been for her. I told her I loved her in a way I'd never loved her before. She didn't move or say anything, but I felt clean and light. I was now free to love her as openly as I could.

"The next morning when I awoke, I was excited to get dressed and visit with her. It was the first time in my life I felt happy to see my mother, really, truly happy. I showered and dressed up so I could look pretty for her. My heart was full of love. I thought of the many things I could tell her and share with her, things that were important to me, things I hadn't told anyone else. As I was walking out of the door, the owner of the nursing home called. Mom had passed in the night.

"I forgave her only hours before she died, and I sometimes wonder if my forgiveness allowed her to pass. I'll never know, of course, but during this time with you, my darling daughter, during our conversations, I've forgiven my mother again—for real this time, in a deep and prayerful way. I feel better now. I think forgiveness comes in waves."

I bent forward and took Mom's hands into mine, caressing them with the same gentleness I had imagined she touched Nonna. "She knew you forgave her. They say that hearing is the last sense to go before death. You set her free, Mom."

"Maybe." She sighed. "That was my prayer."

Then I took a bold step forward. After Dad died, Mom often told me how much she had loved him. Eight years earlier, on Dad's deathbed and minutes before he died, he called her name. She came to his side immediately, climbed into bed next to him, and held him. Her last words to him were, "Please wait for me, Ted. I'll never quit loving you."

But I knew he had hurt her desperately during their life together. I wondered if she could forgive him as she had forgiven her mother.

"Have you forgiven Dad?" I asked gently.

She avoided my eyes by closing hers. "No. Not yet," she responded wearily.

"Mom, do you think you need to forgive him so you can pass?"

A beat of time, and then she said with clarity, "No. I don't think it's necessary that I forgive your father. I'm not sure I can or will. I'll pray about it."

This I understood. It takes time. It took me sixty years.

"But," she interrupted my thoughts with a more confident voice, focusing all her waning energy on me, "I know why the Lord didn't let me pass before this. It was because I had a hole in my heart. The hole was you. But now that you've forgiven me, truly forgiven me, my heart is healed."

That night we followed our bedtime routine: into the wheelchair and into the bathroom. "You sit there," she pointed to a white plastic shower chair near the sink, "while I wash my face and brush my teeth. You're leaving soon and I want you near me every second."

I sat quietly. We didn't talk. Her preparations took her total concentration. As I watched her, I thought about how our roles had reversed. During our final three months together, her gifts of love and courage were huge. I felt privileged and humbled that she allowed me to see her vulnerability, her determination to hang on to her dignity, and her relentless fight against defeat.

When she was back in bed and tucked in for the night, I lay next to her. We had become accustomed to this way of being together. She was on the right and next to the oxygen machine; I was on the left and near the door. We held hands, and I could feel how similar they were, both deeply veined, with bony knuckles and slender fingers. The hands of my nonna too. Three generations blending one into the other.

She was the first to speak.

"Thanks for everything you did for me."

She sounded like a child, innocent and pure, and I thought about what Nonna had told me when I was just seven years old: *Your mamma has the heart of a dove.* Tears streamed down my face and soaked into my hair. No words came, but I nodded my head up and down. She must have felt the movements, two heads sharing one pillow.

"I'm glad we talked about everything," she said softly. Then she continued, "Now you know me." I felt her head nod in a satisfied way. "You finally know me."

My voice choked with sadness, "Why did it take so long, Mom? Why did it take sixty years?"

"Oh," she said softly. "We weren't ready before this."

*

The sea of Rotondella blended into the hills of Pittsburgh, and Nonna came for Mom on December 8, 2012. Four days after my sons and I left the States, on the Feast of the Immaculate Conception, Mom took a breath, exhaled, and let go.

FLORENCE

Chapter 21: Life in Florence

2024

I am in the country of my forebears. Here, the past is with me every day, just as Nonna and Mom are with me every day. There is something about being in Italy that brings them back to me with a gentle, recurring ache.

Nonna comes to me with the sweet scent of tomato sauce as it floats over the music of the Italian language that sets off my longing for her. Maybe it's the steam that fogs my glasses as I drain bubbling hot pasta that returns me to the womb of Nonna's kitchen. Maybe it's the touch of the Arno's soft breeze as it brushes across my cheek that reminds me how much she loved me, from the top of my head to the bottom of my feet.

Mom is more present to me in her absence than she was in her presence. When I hear the deep *bong* of the giant bells of Giotto's tower, I remember her and her unshakable faith. As I ready for bed, I remember how delicately she massaged night cream into her face and neck— always with an upward sweep of her hands and a gentle touch, especially around her eyes. Her eyes, black like the coffee she drank each morning, are what I remember most, especially when, at the end of her life, they radiated tenderness and love for me.

For most of my life, I sold my mother short, putting her into a box labeled *Master of Mixed Messages*. During our last three months together, I came to understand that she had a life before she became my mother, and it was that life that shaped her, hurt her, made her who she was. I wish I had understood this years earlier. She wanted to be tough, resilient, and indomitable, but the wounds from her youth left deep scars that she couldn't erase. I once found a notation in her prayer journal that read, "The demons are back." Is it any wonder that—perhaps tormented all her life by these demons—she was a complicated and contradictory human being, so strong in some situations, so weak in others? How could she have been an easy parent for me?

In the end, she showed incredible courage, for which I'll be forever grateful.

Life brought me back to Italy. Ombretta is still my Louise, and Ferdinando still laughs when we talk about Rotondella. My sons, who live in the States, stay close, call frequently, and visit often. In 2006, Jeff rose out of the ashes of addiction to find his health and spirituality. Jeremy's true calling is as a father to his daughters, Iysabella Carmela and Monroe Avery, whom he parents with gentleness and love.

In 2015, when Iysa was five and preparing for her first trip to Italy, I began telling her stories about Rotondella—the ones my nonna used to tell me. Monroe, born in 2022, is too young to understand, but one day I'll share those memories with her too.

Over the years since Iysa's first visit, I've spoken to her about the strength of her great-great-grandmother, Carmela, who traveled across an ocean to start a new life for her family—how she swept her own sidewalk in the winter wearing only a sweater, made her own wine, canned her own tomatoes, strung her own peppers to dry in the basement, and found edible dandelions for salads in the yard. I've also shared stories of her feisty and independent great-grandmother, Laura, who adored and took care of her daddy and Uncle Jeff.

In my memory, my mother's voice comes back to me: "I wasn't a good mother to you, but I was a good grandmother to your children." From Nonna to me, from my mother to Jeffrey and Jeremy, and now from me to Iysa and Monroe—I hope the circle will continue.

Many years have passed since May 1999, when Ombretta and I made our first visit to Rotondella and found my family. The cousins whom I met then, when our beloved Carmela Perciante was alive, have grown older, as have I, and their children now have children of their own. It's important to me that our connections grow stronger and our history is not lost.

When Iysa visits me each summer, we travel together to the *Mezzogiorno,* to a place once called Lucania. We wind our way up the steep hill to the village of Rotondella, most often accompanied by family, and stand in front of the padlocked door in Via Cervaro. I tell her about the hovel in which Carmela lived, the fields where she labored, and the water that she carried up the mountain.

During her first visit to Rotondella, when Iysa was in first grade, she struggled to understand the significance of this village to her life in America. "Sally, at my school," she questioned me, "came from people who were famous Vikings. Are we famous for anything in Italy besides being poor?"

She's correct that our family's history holds the narrative of poverty, but it also holds the narrative of hard-fought wisdom, pride of achievement, respect for education, love of family, and the dignity of living meaningful lives. I trust that Iysa is developing an understanding of the sacrifices made by those who came before her, on whose shoulders she now stands. The ones who lift her up.

I sometimes wonder what Nonna would say if she saw us now—her granddaughter and great-great granddaughter—back in the bosom of Rotondella. In my quiet moments, I can almost hear her say, "You are crazy, Nonnared. *Ma* I love-a you and you grand-a-babe from t'e top of you head to t'e bottom of you feet."

Iysa, no longer six years old, is now a teenager. The sea, the one too far for Nonna to reach, was Iysa's playground, where she dug in the sand and dove into the gentle waves of the Ionian Sea. She played with her cousins, Beatrice and Lorenzo, and their friends. With them, she felt comfortable and spoke Italian with ease. Under Marilena's patient tutelage, Iysa and her cousin Marco learned to make falaoni just as Nonna did, keeping the traditions of our food alive. With the littlest ones, Chiara and Ilary, she played hide-and-go-seek—that universal game that connects children of all ages. Surrounded by family and love, Iysa is learning to savor the sweet smell of tomato sauce cooking, to feel the brisk and wild sea breeze, and to taste the rich sweetness of apricots and strawberries. Rotondella is weaving its magic for her.

Carmela left Rotondella to start a new life in a new country. Laura turned her back on all things Rotondella; she wanted to be an American and all that that meant. Even as a child, I dreamed of finding Rotondella, but it was not until I was desperate and didn't know where else to turn that I searched it out.

Now Iysa joins this line of women, and we will be her story to pass on. Lives have been lived and lessons learned, by Nonna, by Mom, and by me. We each have our own histories. We each have our own failures. But somehow forgiveness has come at the end and leaves its sweet honey behind.

Rotondella will outlive all of us—a village at the top of a mountain on the instep of the boot of Italy, in the region of Basilicata and the province of Matera. In my head, I hear the church bells of Sant'Antonio ringing. In my imagination, I see Nonna, a young woman, uneducated and inexperienced, as she leaves Rotondella and family behind in the brave hope of a better life for her own children.

Both Carmela and Laura held the same brave hope for a better life for their children and grandchildren. Five days before my mother's death, she asked me:

"My life would make a good book, wouldn't it?"

"But you told me that I wasn't allowed to write about you," I countered.

"After I die, write."

Epilogue

1915

Carmela Perciante's long black wool Sunday dress tangled at her legs when she clambered up into the worn wooden cart. When she was seated, her back straightened and she placed her hands quietly in her lap, palms upward. Her brother, Giuseppe, draped his wool jacket over her shoulders in protection against the chill of the fall morning. He wedged the muslin sack of food Mamma had packed between Carmela's feet. Beside her, where it would be kept safe between them, he placed the cloth bag that held her clothes and the hand-embroidered tablecloth she had made as part of her dowry. The little bag that held her money scratched the skin of her breasts when she shifted her shoulders, to reassure herself that it was safe.

Giuseppe was making a final check of the mule's bindings. Carmela looked at the slices of golden brown and dusty green that marked the wheat fields where the men and women of Rotondella had labored for longer than anyone could say. She did not look around to see her mother, who had to be left behind. Three years earlier, Vincenzo LaGuardia, her husband, had left for l'America, but the money he had saved to send back to her was sufficient only for one. He had promised that in time he would send for her mother, and maybe her sister too.

"I will not be like those others," he'd warned her before he left. "I will not come back to buy the land that ate up my father's life, and his father's before him. I will be an American man. And you will be my American wife."

"I do not believe the streets are paved with gold," she warned him. He shrugged, not a clever man but a strong one, and not given to dreaming.

"But it would be good to eat meat every day," he answered.

"And white bread," she agreed, because that could be true, both the meat and the bread could be available in *l'America*, where a man who knew how to work hard could become rich enough to bring his wife across the ocean to join him and make their lives better.

"I will not be one of those men who disappear forever," he'd promised her, and she had had to believe him. They had known each other all their lives; each knew the quality of the other. He knew he had to leave Rotondella, and she knew that if God spared him, and spared her, he would keep his word.

Her brother climbed into the cart and took his place next to her. He rolled his shoulders back, flicked the reins, and the old mule started to move.

As they pulled away from Rotondella, she heard the choked sobs of her mother, her sister's screams telling her to send money back for her, and the chorus of children's voices as they chased the cart down the hill. They sang the same chorus every time someone left the village: "Portami a *New York*, portami a *New York*."

Head held high, back straight and eyes forward, Carmela never returned to Rotondella. Neither did her daughter. But I do.

Carmela never expected me to weave my way back to her village, to her place of birth. All my life, she had deflected my questions and interest. "I tell you t'ese stories many time. I have no good t'ing to say. T'ey are no good stories." But she had inspired so much in me with her way of being, of protecting, of loving, and of holding our family together. She had given me stories and memories that formed the bridge that finally led me back to her home—and, in many ways, my own.

Acknowledgments

During the summer of 2000, the year after Ombretta and I found family in Rotondella, I started writing this story. When my mother heard about the project, she told me I couldn't write about her. Since she was the critical link between my grandmother and me, I set the writing aside. Twelve years later—just five days before she died—she told me to write. It took several years before I had the clarity to dive back in.

Women need strong female role models, and I had Nonna. My feisty mom—despite all the fraught and difficult moments we lived through—showed incredible courage and vulnerability during her final descent.

Other strong women have entered my life and blessed me. Cynthia Voigt—writer, mentor, and friend—has patiently helped me tell my stories for years. Beena Kamlani, editor, skillfully guided me through many drafts of this book. Lindsay Edgecombe, my former student—now a literary agency executive—continues to believe in me. This adventure never would have happened without Ombretta Ratti, whose determination and care made all the difference.

I offer my deep gratitude to Helene Stapinski, whose family's roots are also in Basilicata, and to Theresa Brown for reading and contributing quotes. Jessica Booth and Randy Ladenheim-Gil also supported me with their expert copyediting skills.

Nicholas Grosso at Bordighera Press was the prince of patience in bringing the manuscript to publication. Thanks also to the Calandra Institute for its vital academic work in advancing Italian American studies. Drs. Anthony Tamburri and Fred Gardaphé are international leaders whose scholarship fosters greater understanding and respect for Italian culture worldwide. I learned a great deal from them, as well as from Drs. David Aliano, Donna Chirico, Roberto Dolci, Daniele Fiorentino, Joe Sciorra, and Sabrina Vellucci.

A heartfelt thanks to my cousins, Ferdinando Risi and Nick Bucci, along with my entire Pittsburgh family, for sharing stories about Nonno Vincenzo, the Black Hand, and what life was like for Italians in the Steel City in the early 1900s.

Thanks to George Burroughs—also a former student and, in spirit, an adopted son—and to Lauren Giordano, who gave generously of their creativity and talent to design the cover and interior sketches.

Thanks to everyone who read and responded to earlier drafts, including Ray Haas—now passed—who was for years my stalwart friend and teacher, as well as Walter Voigt, Ray Hartung, Sue Yiannakis, Anni Hedenig, and Judy MacWilliams. I'm grateful to Patricia Donahue, who offered me her home on a bucolic Maine peninsula, giving me the space to write in beauty and peace.

To my Florentine writer friends—especially Lori Hetherington, Andrea Zurlo, Ciprian Gavriliu, Diedre Pirro's group, and the British Institute's brainstorming group—all of whom offered valuable comments and encouragement.

In the end, it all comes back to family.

To my Florentine family of friends: Alessandra Saviane; Daniela Giannetti; Ioana, Raffaele, Valentina, Adriana, and Donatella Penescu; Kiki and Mauro Annese; Lolita and Frank Savage; Lori and Luca Mattioli; Maria Grazia Locatelli; and Patrisha, Tiberio, and Rebecca Cicali. You sustain me with your friendship and love.

To my Basilicata family—especially Anna, Enrico, Laura, Marilena, Pina, and Claudia, whom we remember always—thank you for opening your hearts to me. Your love and acceptance—and the many meals shared at your table, the same ones Nonna used to cook—have given me comfort and a feeling of home. *Vi voglio bene.*

To my brothers, Ted and JF. We grew up in the same family, even though our memories are sometimes wildly different. Thanks for standing by me through it all. A heartfelt thanks to my older brother, JF, who read an early draft of this story even as he was facing his final chapter.

To Iysa, my oldest granddaughter and travel sidekick to Rotondella, where she is loved by all—especially by me.

Finally, to my sons, Jeff and Jeremy, who are my true inspirations. Jeff, who fought the good fight, is one of the most compassionate, honest, and kind men I know. Jeremy, with his big heart and infectious *anima*, loves with his entire being. My sons are my most avid cheerleaders and steadfast protectors. We three have been through hell and back, but we're still together—and still "staying close."

About the Author

LIBBY CATALDI is an author and former educator who has written about her family's journey through addiction and the legacy of her Italian heritage. She holds a Doctorate in Education from the University of Pittsburgh, co-directed the Maryland Writing Project at Towson University, and was Head of the Calverton School for seventeen years.

The author of *Stay Close* (St. Martin's Press), which was published by Rizzoli as *Stammi Vicino*, she has shared her story widely in the U.S. and Italy, including appearances on NPR, FOX, ABC, RAI Uno, and at the United Nations.

Libby divides her time between Annapolis, Maryland, and Florence, Italy. In Florence, she rowed with the Florence Dragon Boat team for breast cancer survivors, served on the board of the International School of Florence, and is a member of AILO, an organization that supports charitable causes through volunteerism and fundraising. She is also a founding member of the Florence Literary Society.

She is the granddaughter of Italian immigrants and the mother of two sons, whose lives inspired her writing. Learn more at libbycataldi.com.

VIA Folios

A refereed book series dedicated to the culture of Italians and Italian Americans.

DANIELLE JONES. *Hunger*. Vol. 183. Poetry.
GIOSE RIMANELLI. *Benedetta in Guysterland*. Vol. 182. Literature.
DANTE DI STEFANO. *The Widowing Radiance*. Vol. 181. Poetry.
ANNA MONARDO. *The Courtyard of Dreams*. Vol. 180. Novel.
MATTHEW CARIELLO. *Colloquy of Mad Tom*. Vol. 179. Poetry.
GRACE CAVALIERI. *Fables from Italy and Beyond*. Vol. 178. Poetry.
LAURETTE FOLK. *Eleison*. Vol. 177. Novel.
FRANCES NEVILL. *Coquina Soup*. Vol. 176. Literature.
FRANCINE MASIELLO. *The Tomb of the Divers*. Vol. 175. Novel.
PIETRO DI DONATO. *Collected Stories*. Vol. 174. Literature.
RACHEL GUIDO DeVRIES. *The Birthday Years*. Vol. 173. Poetry.
MATTHEW MEDURI. *Collegiate Gothic*. Vol. 172. Novel.
THOMAS RUGGIO. *Finding Dandini*. Vol. 171. Art History.
TAMBURRI GIORDANO GARDAPHÈ. *From the Margin*. Vol. 170. Anthology.
ANNA MONARDO. *After Italy*. Vol. 169. Memoir.
JOEY NICOLETTI. *Extinction Wednesday*. Vol. 168. Poetry.
MARIA FAMÀ. *Trigger*. Vol. 167. Poetry.
WILLI Q MINN. *What? Nothing*. Vol. 166. Poetry.
RICHARD VETERE. *She's Not There*. Vol. 165. Literature.
FRANK GIOIA. *Mercury Man*. Vol. 164. Literature.
LUISA M. GIULIANETTI. *Agrodolce*. Vol. 163. Literature.
ANGELO ZEOLLA. *The Bronx Unbound ovvero i versi bronxesi*. Vol. 162. Poetry.
NICHOLAS A. DiCHARIO. *Giovanni's Tree*. Vol. 161. Literature.
ADELE ANNESI. *What She Takes Away*. Vol. 160. Novel.
ANNIE RACHELE LANZILLOTTO. *Whaddyacall the Wind?*. Vol. 159. Memoir.
JULIA LISELLA. *Our Lively Kingdom*. Vol. 158. Poetry.
MARK CIABATTARI. *When the Mask Slips*. Vol. 157. Novel.
JENNIFER MARTELLI. *The Queen of Queens*. Vol. 156. Poetry.
TONY TADDEI. *The Sons of the Santorelli*. Vol. 155. Literature.
FRANCO RICCI. *Preston Street • Corso Italias*. Vol. 154. History.
MIKE FIORITO. *The Hated Ones*. Vol. 153. Literature.
PATRICIA DUNN. *Last Stop on the 6*. Vol. 152. Novel.
WILLIAM BOELHOWER. *Immigrant Autobiography*. Vol. 151. Literary Criticism.
MARC DIPAOLO. *Fake Italian*. Vol. 150. Literature.
GAIL REITANO. *Italian Love Cake*. Vol. 149. Novel.
VINCENT PANELLA. *Sicilian Dreams*. Vol. 148. Novel.
MARK CIABATTARI. *The Literal Truth: Rizzoli Dreams of Eating the Apple of Earthly Delights*. Vol. 147. Novel.
MARK CIABATTARI. *Dreams of An Imaginary New Yorker Named Rizzoli*. Vol. 146. Novel.
LAURETTE FOLK. *The End of Aphrodite*. Vol. 145. Novel.
ANNA CITRINO. *A Space Between*. Vol. 144. Poetry

MARIA FAMÀ. *The Good for the Good*. Vol. 143. Poetry.
ROSEMARY CAPPELLO. *Wonderful Disaster*. Vol. 142. Poetry.
B. AMORE. *Journeys on the Wheel*. Vol. 141. Poetry.
ALDO PALAZZESCHI. *The Manifestos of Aldo Palazzeschi*. Vol 140. Literature.
ROSS TALARICO. *The Reckoning*. Vol 139. Poetry.
MICHELLE REALE. *Season of Subtraction*. Vol 138. Poetry.
MARISA FRASCA. *Wild Fennel*. Vol 137. Poetry.
RITA ESPOSITO WATSON. *Italian Kisses*. Vol. 136. Memoir.
SARA FRUNER. *Bitter Bites from Sugar Hills*. Vol. 135. Poetry.
KATHY CURTO. *Not for Nothing*. Vol. 134. Memoir.
JENNIFER MARTELLI. *My Tarantella*. Vol. 133. Poetry.
MARIA TERRONE. *At Home in the New World*. Vol. 132. Essays.
GIL FAGIANI. *Missing Madonnas*. Vol. 131. Poetry.
LEWIS TURCO. *The Sonnetarium*. Vol. 130. Poetry.
JOE AMATO. *Samuel Taylor's Hollywood Adventure*. Vol. 129. Novel.
BEA TUSIANI. *Con Amore*. Vol. 128. Memoir.
MARIA GIURA. *What My Father Taught Me*. Vol. 127. Poetry.
STANISLAO PUGLIESE. *A Century of Sinatra*. Vol. 126. Popular Culture.
TONY ARDIZZONE. *The Arab's Ox*. Vol. 125. Novel.
PHYLLIS CAPELLO. *Packs Small Plays Big*. Vol. 124. Literature.
FRED GARDAPHÉ. *Read 'em and Reap*. Vol. 123. Criticism.
JOSEPH A. AMATO. *Diagnostics*. Vol 122. Literature.
DENNIS BARONE. *Second Thoughts*. Vol 121. Poetry.
OLIVIA K. CERRONE. *The Hunger Saint*. Vol 120. Novella.
GARIBLADI M. LAPOLLA. *Miss Rollins in Love*. Vol 119. Novel.
JOSEPH TUSIANI. *A Clarion Call*. Vol 118. Poetry.
JOSEPH A. AMATO. *My Three Sicilies*. Vol 117. Poetry & Prose.
MARGHERITA COSTA. *Voice of a Virtuosa and Coutesan*. Vol 116. Poetry.
NICOLE SANTALUCIA. *Because I Did Not Die*. Vol 115. Poetry.
MARK CIABATTARI. *Preludes to History*. Vol 114. Poetry.
HELEN BAROLINI. *Visits*. Vol 113. Novel.
ERNESTO LIVORNI. *The Fathers' America*. Vol 112. Poetry.
MARIO B. MIGNONE. *The Story of My People*. Vol 111. Non-fiction.
GEORGE GUIDA. *The Sleeping Gulf*. Vol 110. Poetry.
JOEY NICOLETTI. *Reverse Graffiti*. Vol 109. Poetry.
GIOSE RIMANELLI. *Il mestiere del furbo*. Vol 108. Criticism.
LEWIS TURCO. *The Hero Enkidu*. Vol 107. Poetry.
AL TACCONELLI. *Perhaps Fly*. Vol 106. Poetry.
RACHEL GUIDO DEVRIES. *A Woman Unknown in Her Bones*. Vol 105. Poetry.
BERNARD BRUNO. *A Tear and a Tear in My Heart*. Vol 104. Non-fiction.
FELIX STEFANILE. *Songs of the Sparrow*. Vol 103. Poetry.
FRANK POLIZZI. *A New Life with Bianca*. Vol 102. Poetry.
GIL FAGIANI. *Stone Walls*. Vol 101. Poetry.
LOUISE DESALVO. *Casting Off*. Vol 100. Fiction.
MARY JO BONA. *I Stop Waiting for You*. Vol 99. Poetry.
RACHEL GUIDO DEVRIES. *Stati zitt, Josie*. Vol 98. Children's Literature. $8

GRACE CAVALIERI. *The Mandate of Heaven*. Vol 97. Poetry.
MARISA FRASCA. *Via incanto*. Vol 96. Poetry.
DOUGLAS GLADSTONE. *Carving a Niche for Himself.* Vol 95. History.
MARIA TERRONE. *Eye to Eye*. Vol 94. Poetry.
CONSTANCE SANCETTA. *Here in Cerchio*. Vol 93. Local History.
MARIA MAZZIOTTI GILLAN. *Ancestors' Song*. Vol 92. Poetry.
MICHAEL PARENTI. *Waiting for Yesterday: Pages from a Street Kid's Life*. Vol 90. Memoir.
ANNIE LANZILLOTTO. *Schistsong*. Vol 89. Poetry.
EMANUEL DI PASQUALE. *Love Lines*. Vol 88. Poetry.
CAROSONE & LOGIUDICE. *Our Naked Lives*. Vol 87. Essays.
JAMES PERICONI. *Strangers in a Strange Land: A Survey of Italian-Language American Books*. Vol 86. Book History.
DANIELA GIOSEFFI. *Escaping La Vita Della Cucina*. Vol 85. Essays.
MARIA FAMÀ. *Mystics in the Family*. Vol 84. Poetry.
ROSSANA DEL ZIO. *From Bread and Tomatoes to Zuppa di Pesce "Ciambotto"*. Vol. 83. Memoir.
LORENZO DELBOCA. *Polentoni*. Vol 82. Italian Studies.
SAMUEL GHELLI. *A Reference Grammar*. Vol 81. Italian Language.
ROSS TALARICO. *Sled Run*. Vol 80. Fiction.
FRED MISURELLA. *Only Sons*. Vol 79. Fiction.
FRANK LENTRICCHIA. *The Portable Lentricchia*. Vol 78. Fiction.
RICHARD VETERE. *The Other Colors in a Snow Storm*. Vol 77. Poetry.
GARIBALDI LAPOLLA. *Fire in the Flesh*. Vol 76 Fiction & Criticism.
GEORGE GUIDA. *The Pope Stories*. Vol 75 Prose.
ROBERT VISCUSI. *Ellis Island*. Vol 74. Poetry.
ELENA GIANINI BELOTTI. *The Bitter Taste of Strangers Bread*. Vol 73. Fiction.
PINO APRILE. *Terroni*. Vol 72. Italian Studies.
EMANUEL DI PASQUALE. *Harvest*. Vol 71. Poetry.
ROBERT ZWEIG. *Return to Naples*. Vol 70. Memoir.
AIROS & CAPPELLI. *Guido*. Vol 69. Italian/American Studies.
FRED GARDAPHÉ. *Moustache Pete is Dead! Long Live Moustache Pete!*. Vol 67. Literature/Oral History.
PAOLO RUFFILLI. *Dark Room/Camera oscura*. Vol 66. Poetry.
HELEN BAROLINI. *Crossing the Alps*. Vol 65. Fiction.
COSMO FERRARA. *Profiles of Italian Americans*. Vol 64. Italian Americana.
GIL FAGIANI. *Chianti in Connecticut*. Vol 63. Poetry.
BASSETTI & D'ACQUINO. *Italic Lessons*. Vol 62. Italian/American Studies.
CAVALIERI & PASCARELLI, Eds. *The Poet's Cookbook*. Vol 61. Poetry/Recipes.
EMANUEL DI PASQUALE. *Siciliana*. Vol 60. Poetry.
NATALIA COSTA, Ed. *Bufalini*. Vol 59. Poetry.
RICHARD VETERE. *Baroque*. Vol 58. Fiction.
LEWIS TURCO. *La Famiglia/The Family*. Vol 57. Memoir.
NICK JAMES MILETI. *The Unscrupulous*. Vol 56. Humanities.
BASSETTI. ACCOLLA. D'AQUINO. *Italici: An Encounter with Piero Bassetti*. Vol 55. Italian Studies.

GIOSE RIMANELLI. *The Three-legged One*. Vol 54. Fiction.
CHARLES KLOPP. *Bele Antiche Stòrie*. Vol 53. Criticism.
JOSEPH RICAPITO. *Second Wave*. Vol 52. Poetry.
GARY MORMINO. *Italians in Florida*. Vol 51. History.
GIANFRANCO ANGELUCCI. *Federico F*. Vol 50. Fiction.
ANTHONY VALERIO. *The Little Sailor*. Vol 49. Memoir.
ROSS TALARICO. *The Reptilian Interludes*. Vol 48. Poetry.
RACHEL GUIDO DE VRIES. *Teeny Tiny Tino's Fishing Story*.
   Vol 47. Children's Literature.
EMANUEL DI PASQUALE. *Writing Anew*. Vol 46. Poetry.
MARIA FAMÀ. *Looking For Cover*. Vol 45. Poetry.
ANTHONY VALERIO. *Toni Cade Bambara's One Sicilian Night*. Vol 44. Poetry.
EMANUEL CARNEVALI. *Furnished Rooms*. Vol 43. Poetry.
BRENT ADKINS. et al., Ed. *Shifting Borders. Negotiating Places*.
   Vol 42. Conference.
GEORGE GUIDA. *Low Italian*. Vol 41. Poetry.
GARDAPHÈ, GIORDANO, TAMBURRI. *Introducing Italian Americana*.
   Vol 40. Italian/American Studies.
DANIELA GIOSEFFI. *Blood Autumn/Autunno di sangue*. Vol 39. Poetry.
FRED MISURELLA. *Lies to Live By*. Vol 38. Stories.
STEVEN BELLUSCIO. *Constructing a Bibliography*. Vol 37. Italian Americana.
ANTHONY JULIAN TAMBURRI, Ed. *Italian Cultural Studies 2002*.
   Vol 36. Essays.
BEA TUSIANI. *con amore*. Vol 35. Memoir.
FLAVIA BRIZIO-SKOV, Ed. *Reconstructing Societies in the Aftermath of War*.
   Vol 34. History.
TAMBURRI. et al., Eds. *Italian Cultural Studies 2001*. Vol 33. Essays.
ELIZABETH G. MESSINA, Ed. *In Our Own Voices*.
   Vol 32. Italian/American Studies.
STANISLAO G. PUGLIESE. *Desperate Inscriptions*. Vol 31. History.
HOSTERT & TAMBURRI, Eds. *Screening Ethnicity*.
   Vol 30. Italian/American Culture.
G. PARATI & B. LAWTON, Eds. *Italian Cultural Studies*. Vol 29. Essays.
HELEN BAROLINI. *More Italian Hours*. Vol 28. Fiction.
FRANCO NASI, Ed. *Intorno alla Via Emilia*. Vol 27. Culture.
ARTHUR L. CLEMENTS. *The Book of Madness & Love*. Vol 26. Poetry.
JOHN CASEY, et al. *Imagining Humanity*. Vol 25. Interdisciplinary Studies.
ROBERT LIMA. *Sardinia/Sardegna*. Vol 24. Poetry.
DANIELA GIOSEFFI. *Going On*. Vol 23. Poetry.
ROSS TALARICO. *The Journey Home*. Vol 22. Poetry.
EMANUEL DI PASQUALE. *The Silver Lake Love Poems*. Vol 21. Poetry.
JOSEPH TUSIANI. *Ethnicity*. Vol 20. Poetry.
JENNIFER LAGIER. *Second Class Citizen*. Vol 19. Poetry.
FELIX STEFANILE. *The Country of Absence*. Vol 18. Poetry.
PHILIP CANNISTRARO. *Blackshirts*. Vol 17. History.
LUIGI RUSTICHELLI, Ed. *Seminario sul racconto*. Vol 16. Narrative.

LEWIS TURCO. *Shaking the Family Tree.* Vol 15. Memoirs.
LUIGI RUSTICHELLI, Ed. *Seminario sulla drammaturgia.*
  Vol 14. Theater/Essays.
FRED GARDAPHÈ. *Moustache Pete is Dead! Long Live Moustache Pete!.*
  Vol 13. Oral Literature.
JONE GAILLARD CORSI. *Il libretto d'autore. 1860 - 1930.* Vol 12. Criticism.
HELEN BAROLINI. *Chiaroscuro: Essays of Identity.* Vol 11. Essays.
PICARAZZI & FEINSTEIN, Eds. *An African Harlequin in Milan.*
  Vol 10. Theater/Essays.
JOSEPH RICAPITO. *Florentine Streets & Other Poems.* Vol 9. Poetry.
FRED MISURELLA. *Short Time.* Vol 8. Novella.
NED CONDINI. *Quartettsatz.* Vol 7. Poetry.
ANTHONY JULIAN TAMBURRI, Ed. *Fuori: Essays by Italian/American Lesbiansand Gays.* Vol 6. Essays.
ANTONIO GRAMSCI. P. Verdicchio. Trans. & Intro. *The Southern Question.*
  Vol 5. Social Criticism.
DANIELA GIOSEFFI. *Word Wounds & Water Flowers.* Vol 4. Poetry. $8
WILEY FEINSTEIN. *Humility's Deceit: Calvino Reading Ariosto Reading Calvino.*
  Vol 3. Criticism.
PAOLO A. GIORDANO, Ed. *Joseph Tusiani: Poet. Translator. Humanist.*
  Vol 2. Criticism.
ROBERT VISCUSI. *Oration Upon the Most Recent Death of Christopher Columbus.*
  Vol 1. Poetry.

www.ingramcontent.com/pod-product-compliance
Lightning Source LLC
Chambersburg PA
CBHW030854170426
43193CB00009BA/608